Love Notes

"Amazing! Impactful each of Dayan's 7 steps is unbeatable, brimming with wisdom, enthusiasm and inspiration. Get this one-of-a-kind book and be ready to get The Power to Reinvent your Life and fuel your success!"

– Robert G. Allen, New York Times Bestselling author, Speaker, Investment Advisor, Author of *One Minute Millionaire*

"Yvonne's 7 unbeatable steps to Reinvent Your Life are practical, simple, yet the powerful ideas you'll get from them will amaze you! Get this book and begin to live your best life!"

– Donovan S. Gray, LCSW, Licensed Clinical Social Work

"In the personal development world, Yvonne is a rare and worldly treasure. Through her writings and seminars, she gets the message across about how important it is to constantly update and evolve into a higher version of ourselves. This book is a blue print to help empower yourself."

– Cynthia Sharp, Esquire, Business Development Expert

"Whatever Yvonne Dayan says or writes, I want to listen intently, and I promise, you'll want to listen, too. She can transform deep, mystical concepts into simple tools for success and daily living. Her book is filled with wisdom that you'll be able to put it to work in your life right away. I highly recommend this book as well as any of her courses!"

– Eddie Lara, Video & Photographer

"In another time when I was lost, I met Yvonne and had the good fortune to read her book, as well as participate in her Course. Through my 360-degree turn in my life, I found peace, health, prosperity, happiness, and spirituality. I now see the brighter side of life and success comes easy to me. I encourage everyone to absorb the strategies in this book, and don't miss out on her reinvention course; It's well worth gold! "

– Stella Bermudez, Director of the Smarlin Corporation

"*Yvonne Dayan has the genius ability to help people find and realize their passion. She helped me reinvent myself more than once and helped me find my passion and harness my abilities to reach new heights in my career. I wish for everyone to live their passion as I do and this book will help you do just that. Highly recommended, especially for loving your life and getting to your next level of success!*"

– Yulie Heaton, Director of Yulie's Yoga

"*I've always believed Yvonne is one of the most talented teachers in the personal development world today. Her book is a testimony of her knowledge on how to maximize our personal and business potential through taking our life to the next level.*"

– Narda Urrea, CEO of Technology Entrepreneurial Services

"The Power to Reinvent Your Life *will become a classic in your library. Yvonne Dayan's philosophy for reinvention is timeless, and her principles are practical and Universal. You'll learn to become fearless, live your highest vision of yourself, and more.*"

– Conrado Gomez, Director of Shiatsu Colombia

"*"Amazing, Creative, Relevant… a game-changer to get women like me back into their Inner Power. I not only gained the steps I was missing, I also got motivated to make changes. I've reinvented my financial success and am enjoying financial freedom. The results I've had by learning about reinvention and working personally with Yvonne and her team have renewed and enriched my soul!*"

– Alba Luz Henao, Business Administration Expert

"*In this world of fear and doubt, Yvonne Dayan's powerful messages always leaves me feeling motivated, uplifted and equipped with practical tools to achieve success. The Power to Reinvent Your Life is another amazing resource to keep handy. Thanks Yvonne!*"

– Lina Morales, United Health International

"Fabulous! Creative! What a way to get women back into their Power. Yvonne is a true master in reinventing any area of life and transforming defeat into real Success. I will use the strategies in her book at home and in the workplace in many ways. I highly recommend you get it, do it, and enjoy it!"

— Carmela Soussa, Secretary

A simple, short, and brilliant road map to get you from where you are to where you want to be, Yvonne shares her wisdom and insights."

— Ahitza Gonzales, Judge, ESQ

*"*The Power to Reinvent Your Life *is an invitation to improve your life, so that you can experience the Freedom to be the best version of yourself. Do yourself and your business a favor and accept this invitation. Then, enjoy the journey as these steps guide you and reignite your life."*

— Mollie Reckley

"I Reinvented myself and took my relationships to the next level. My life has improved immensely following Yvonne Dayan's blueprint. This book is like a powerful rare gem. **Get it, Read it and Take the steps she prescribes.***"*

— Ana Watkin, CEO of Shefa Designs

"Yvonne Dayan's concept of Reinvention is pure Genius. I've reinvented myself and I now know how to take care of all of **Me**. *My way of eating and relationship to food has improved dramatically. I HAVE PASSION to go for the things I really want. I feel lucky to belong to this Inner Forte™ family of awesome, loving, and supportive people! Yvonne and her team are the 'Real Thing.' Get this book and get your life on board!"*

— Dilcia Cabral, Administrator

"I've been taking Yvonne's courses for over 15 years; my life keeps getting better, and my confidence is sky high as a result, and I want more!"

— Dilia Rodriguez, Accountant

THE POWER TO REINVENT YOUR LIFE

7 Steps for Jumpstarting Your Passion, Purpose, and Success

THE POWER TO REINVENT YOUR LIFE

7 Steps for Jumpstarting Your Passion, Purpose, and Success

YVONNE DAYAN

The Power to Reinvent Your Life: 7 Steps for Jumpstarting Your Passion, Purpose, and Success

By Yvonne Dayan

Published 2019 by Aledi Publishing Group, www.AlediPublishing.com

The contents of this book and the author make no claims, guarantees or warranties as to the suitability of any of the self-help secrets, steps, keys, strategies, technologies, techniques, tools, exercises, advice, material, etc. contained herein which may or may not be suitable or appropriate for the specific situation or person who, at the particular moment in time, may or not be physically, emotionally, mentally, spiritually or psychologically prepared to either adopt and/or practice any of the material in this book and/or handle any of the consequences as a result thereof. The reader is herewith advised to consult with a medical doctor, a professional psychotherapist, psychologist or psychiatrist, as may be appropriate, before applying any of the strategies, exercises or advice mentioned in this book. All information and statements made in this book are the personal experience and opinion of the author and are not meant as, nor do they constitute, personal or business consulting or personal counseling of any kind. Neither the publisher nor the author are engaged in rendering professional services, and the reader should consult with a professional where appropriate. Neither the author nor the publisher shall be liable for any loss or damages, including but not limited to special, incidental, consequential, or other damages resulting from the use of any of the information and data in this book. The intent of the author is only to offer information of a general nature to help you in your quest for appreciation of and learning about the inherent power that we as evolving beings have to reinvent our lives in many forms.

ISBN 978-0-9771445-6-3 (Hardback)
ISBN 978-0-9771445-7-0 (Paperback)
ISBN 978-0-9771445-9-4 (Ebook)

1. Motivational & Inspirational, 2. Personal Growth/Success, 3. Personal Growth/Happiness
1 3 5 7 9 10 8 6 4 2
Cover and interior design by Julia McMinn Evans
Social Media Logo vectors created by alicia_mb, www.freepik.com

For more information about personalized editions, special seminars, speaking events and corporate discounts please contact us at info@innerforte.com.

www.innerforte.com

DEDICATION

May this book encourage you to transform your life to be your best, have the best, and give your best always and in all ways!

I dedicate this book to my mother, the best role model and most vivid example for reinvention, who by her example inspires me and all the lucky ones who know her, to BELIEVE, to DARE to live in the POSSIBILTIES, always full of optimism, and commitment to loving abundantly, and giving from the heart; who never lets me stay the same, and positively has challenged me through the years to live boldly and reach my highest potential.

And first and foremost, to My Creator, who loves and reinvents me together with all of creation every single day!

CONTENTS

PREFACE

The Rewards of Reinvention

In any effort to improve your life, it's important to understand what you stand to gain—and why it's worth the effort.

In a world where chaos reigns, where terrorism, violence, crime, and disease are almost the norm, anyone can still reinvent their life positively, and by doing so, impact others by their own example. It is not a hopeless world; it depends on us. We are powerful beings, each like a pebble in a pond. By our change, we can impact our surroundings, empower others to change and reinvent their lives, and even act as change agents to transform our world.

With that in mind, here are **five powerful benefits** you will enjoy when you successfully reinvent your life:

1. Reinvention unlocks potential

Putting yourself on the path to reinvention brings with it the likelihood of reaching your full potential. You will find yourself opening your mind to fresh and exciting possibilities you could not have conceived of before, possibilities centered around new breakthroughs and accomplishments which reflect your unique talents and most cherished dreams.

2. Reinvention gives you power

When you dare to crack out of your cocoon like a butterfly, you take on new wings to fly that lift you up and transform your life. You feel empowered in a way you never imagined. That power energizes your everyday life and gives it its purpose.

3. Reinvention compels you to pursue your passion

Ever feel like you're sleepwalking through life? You won't any longer if you pursue reinvention. Suddenly, you are in touch with your deepest passions and desires and they motivate you to make new decisions and goals that excite you, rather than exhaust you.

4. Reinvention recharges your "zest for life."

Being in touch with your passions will inevitably give you a renewed zest for living, and for finding professional, personal and spiritual fulfillment. You no longer feel stuck—instead, you will be consumed with finding ways to make magical things happen in your life. With a new love for life, you learn to value, appreciate, and love yourself for who you are.

5. Reinvention develops your Inner Forte™.

Your Inner Forte™ is the powerful Force Within that unlocks your natural strengths and empowers you to take the leap of faith required for reinvention. It puts you in touch with your Higher Intuitive Self and helps you take bold new steps that align with your values and purpose. That, in turn, enables you to achieve greatness and lasting fulfillment in your life.

Reinventing your life is not easy. It means making significant and potentially difficult changes that will ultimately lead to your bliss. In this book, you'll find a step-by-step approach to create your own meaningful reinvention journey...and discover your most authentic and fulfilling life!

INTRODUCTION

*You are the star in the story of your life;
why not...give it your all and reinvent now!*
Yvonne Dayan

You are strong, powerful, intelligent and capable of doing any-thing that you put your mind to. You were born to be happy, to triumph, and to thrive!

I know it doesn't always feel that way. When life takes an unexpected turn, everything can seem confusing and discourag-ing. Throughout the hustle and bustle of daily life, you may find yourself being spread too thin, overshadowed by others who have too much power over your decisions, spending your time and energy on things that matter little, and feeling your inner fire diminishing and your passion ebbing. It takes its toll and you can easily find yourself forgetting who you really are and what powerful things you are capable of.

As you'll see in this book, these moments of upheaval are often opportunities in disguise, turning points where you can make a fresh start, choose a new path or get back in touch with dreams you had abandoned. These moments may happen after you've experienced some kind of traumatic loss or reached a crossroads in your life when you must make an important choice. Most success stories of life reinvention occur during challenging and changing times, times when you have the power to begin creating a better you, when you can reshape your dreams into a future you are meant to bring forth, both for yourself and those around you.

Each one of us has the power to take the aspects of our life that are no longer moving us forward but, instead, holding us back, and redesign them. When we recognize that we have that power and use it correctly, then our own life reinvention truly becomes possible.

I know this first hand, as I've reinvented my life and career several times during this lifetime. This book is a result of those experiences and the knowledge realized from my own journey, plus the results of my beloved students.

My first reinvention, which was necessitated after my divorce, was the most painful and perhaps the most crucial one. I was on a downward spiral that felt endless—I had lost everything, including my social status, and what I had felt was my place in the world. This, in turn, made me feel powerless to do anything, have anything and even be anything— my passion and my sense of self seemed to have vanished along with any hope for improvement. I was low on confidence and money and high on uncertainty and fear, mostly about the future of my family. I knew I needed some kind of radical change, since almost everything I had done up until that point obviously did not work.

My turning point in my quest for reinvention came when I finally allowed myself to question certain beliefs that were an intrinsic part of the culture I had grown up in. When I began to redefine my role in the world according to what I believed, I was able to also redefine what success was for me – both in a personal and professional sense. Stepping out of my previous mental 'box' was the all-important first step in my reinvention that took on the road to happiness, fulfillment, and life satisfaction.

Reigniting Your Fire

Perhaps you're in a similar position to where I was. Perhaps you're looking for a big, positive and sweeping life change. On the other hand, maybe you're not looking for massive change—

maybe there are only a few specific areas of your life you feel need addressing.

Whatever your situation, these 7 Reinvention Steps I will be revealing in this book can help you with your goals. These are the same steps and principles I used to achieve success and empower not only myself, but also the tens of thousands of people I've joyfully trained and coached over the years, both individually and in group settings.

The strategies for completing all 7 of these steps are explained briefly in this book. In the near future, however, I will be expanding on these steps and revealing 21 more lessons for personal transformation in my online video course, *Unlocking Your Inner Forte™ - 21 Keys to Reinvent Your Best Life Ever*.

Again, all of these tools are based on my own experiences and my own studies in helping others live the purposeful and passion-filled life we all crave and deserve. Perhaps the most important lesson I've learned over the years is that we work the hardest and feel the most passion when we are striving towards something that is *bigger than ourselves*. I felt that power myself while creating these life reinvention tools— because what fires me up more than anything else is my mission to help others reconnect with themselves and live their ultimate purpose.

Change Never Stops

I know that life wants all of us to continually reinvent ourselves and to use that reinvention process to increase our passion, our drive and our perfection. We should all strive to become the best version of who we can be. But to get as close to that goal as possible, we need to focus and we need to act. This book is designed to help you do all that and more, so you can achieve what you want out of life with joy and ease.

Each step and strategy is designed to progressively move you along your own transformational journey. Each is filled with inspiring ideas, thought-provoking choices and amazing opportunities to recharge and rejuvenate your spirit. If you want to jumpstart your own journey towards living a more meaningful and joyful life, if you want to grow beyond past traumas and setbacks and enjoy a new level of passion and success, this book will give you the tools that will enable you to realize all that.

You'll also find that when losses, disappointments and challenges cause you to feel less than your ideal self, you can regain your confidence and power and move yourself forward towards reinvention. And as you proceed forward, you'll find yourself uncovering untapped strengths and talents and opening up new possibilities for realizing your dreams in a way that matters to your most Authentic Self. This book will also help you gain a deeper sense of purpose, which will allow you to truly prosper in every area of your life, and even become a beacon of light to others facing their own struggles.

If you look all around you, reinvention is a constant in our changing world. From the largest multinational corporation to the smallest mom-and-pop business, innovation has to be a constant for business survival. Car models are updated and added to on a yearly basis and technology is always bringing us new and exciting breakthroughs. Even the food we eat is always changing, as chefs find amazing new ways to create dishes we've never seen (or tasted!) before.

Change is a constant all around us—and it should be a constant within us as well. Through an ongoing reinvention process, we can create the best version of ourselves and enjoy an amazing amount of passion and pleasure along the way! Each of our 'upgrades' will outperform the earlier versions of ourselves, until we reach the point where we can prosper outrageously, love abundantly and heal all our past wounds once and for all. This has been my experience and it's an experience I want you to savor and enjoy as well!

Are You Ready to Reinvent?

It took time to develop the concepts in this book—some of them came, I admit, painfully slow, others with lightning-fast speed—but once I translated my flashes of inspiration into the 7 steps you're about to read, *everything* became clear. And now I can share this blueprint for reinvention with not only you, but with the world.

I truly encourage you to not only read this book, but also take the time to reflect on each of the 7 steps and each of the 50+ strategies I've included with those steps until you **assimilate** them and **extract** their alchemy by acting on them in your daily life. For best results, once you read the entire book and practice the 7 steps, simply pick a strategy of your preference to use daily or as needed and practice it until you gain mastery over it. Then, continue to explore and play with the myriad ways you can apply them to your personal life and business endeavors.

So, prepare yourself as we journey together through these 7 adventurous steps, which will empower you to:

1. **Exert Your Power of Choice to Reinvent Your Life**

2. **Create Your Great and Unifying Vision**

3. **Jumpstart Your Mind for Success**

4. **Trust Yourself (You've Got What It Takes!)**

5. **Build the Courage to Shake Off Setbacks**

6. **Get Creative as You Explore New Passions**

7. **Commit to See Your Reinvention Through**

It's time you find your purpose once again. Now is when you should fire up whatever fuels your passion and allow it to take control of your future. It's time to step into your greatness, and unlock that Unlimited Force, that *Inner Forte™* within you that sits in the center of your being, capable of achieving much more than what you give it credit for.

It's time to shine your brightest as you roll out the best version of yourself. And it all happens on your journey to reinvent your life.

This book is charged with positive energy, which I've reinforced with inspiring quotes, all of them based on my own experience and inspiration, which you will find framed throughout the book. I encourage you to keep it next to your bed and in your desk in the office to fill yourself up with energy instantaneously!

As a bonus to my readers, this book can also be used as a 'Guide.' When you need an answer to a particular situation, just ask yourself a question, then… open the book at random, and you will find an idea that will help guide you towards your highest good!

Enjoy!

Yvonne Dayan

CHAPTER 1

Exerting the Power of Choice

The first step in changing and transforming your life is
realizing that Choice is a Life-altering Power.
Yvonne Dayan

Whenever you're faced with a big challenge in your life, remember, you have **three choices**: You can (1) let it define you, (2) allow it to destroy you, or… (3) Let it inspire you to make the next right choice to *Reinvent Your Life*.

We all have the Power of Choice to make positive changes in our lives.

Reinventing yourself requires, more than anything else, making the right choices (for you) that will motivate you to positively change your life and your surroundings. And as *you* change, the world around you will also inevitably change. This empowering idea works so well because while many go about forcing change on other people or situations with no results, this way of thinking demonstrates that we can insure ourselves peace, prosperity, and jumpstart our success by choosing to make changes within ourselves first.

When you make your choices, you own the results—and you can see what those results will bring into your life—whether positive or negative; small or large, taking bold steps to make a stand for yourself, in the direction of your goals is empowering and you can always *expect the best!*

Your reinvention depends upon your ability to accept the outcomes of your choices with grace and to remember that what seems at times to be a negative result most often ends up being an amazingly positive opportunity in disguise.

Circumstances, people, and unexpected situations can cause us to alter our course, overwhelm us, and make us feel as though we have no control over our own future. We lose confidence in our judgment and capabilities, we abandon our dreams and, instead, return to doing what's 'safe.' Or, worse, we allow others to determine our personal destiny.

When that happens, it's because we've lost self-confidence in our ability to make the right choices for ourselves. The truth is, we always have choices available, and it's empowering for us to know the things we can change and take responsibility for our own choices. For example:

- The choice of what to give your attention to is yours.
- The choice to change and grow is yours.
- The choice to be happy is yours.
- The choice to set new goals is yours.
- The choice to eat well and care for your health is yours.
- The choice to exercise and love your body is yours.
- The choice to forgive and heal is yours.
- The choice to be successful and prosper no matter what outer appearances dictate is yours.

- The choice to hate or to love is yours.
- The choice to choose whether the glass is half empty or half full is yours.
- The choice to listen and trust Your Unlimited Source is yours,
- The choice to expect the worse or to believe the best is yet to come is always yours.

Choices are unlimited opportunities which are available to us all the time! They keep our attention directed towards the things that we can develop, thus advancing us to our next level.

Yes, this power is within all of us, and exerting it is the first step towards making the changes that will bring you the happiness and success we all deserve. When we expect the best and affirm our best, we also attract the best outcomes to follow us throughout our reinvention journey.

To start using this power, and reap the rewards, start affirming these positive ideas about reinvention, and you will start seeing amazing opportunities of all kinds draw near to you. Choosing positive thoughts and positive words to declare something you want opens up unlimited opportunities, raises your mood instantly, and sets you up for success! So go ahead and declare your Reinvention affirmations with passion and power NOW!

- Today I choose to believe in me, and in my Power to Reinvent my life anew every day!
- I have the power to make positive and healthy choices that produce excellent results!
- I choose to only 'speak' health, wealth, and happiness, and see them happening in my life and in the life of others!

DETERMINE YOUR DIRECTION

The choices we make allow us to select which direction we want our lives to take—the what, why and how. And that ability to improve the quality of our lives is the single most amazing gift we receive from The Force of The Universe.

This is the gift of free will, to improve our lives, or to destroy it. Free will is our power to choose a course of action that genuinely affects our destiny. It's a waste not to use that gift to the fullest!

To start putting the Power of Choice to work in your life, take some time to consider these three important questions and answer them honestly to reflect where you are in your life:

1. **Do you direct the course of your life?**

2. **Are you currently the best version of yourself?**

3. **Are you where you want to be?**

If you answered no to any of these questions, then now is the time for you to begin your own personal reinvention process. Now is the time to understand that you can transform your life, or any part of it and become the best, truest, and most fulfilled version of yourself.

I've seen it happen for myself by experience, training, and helping others from around the world to achieve their life and career reinvention. It's always truly a joy to witness them go beyond their day-to-day struggles to living successful and purpose-filled lives—and see them accomplish all of this in relatively short periods of time.

These are people who came from all walks of life, all ages, languages and beliefs systems, and from all levels of society. They range from powerful executives and entrepreneurs to those

weakened from battling sickness and addiction; from the emo-
tionally-distraught coping with traumatic divorces and break-
ups to single women seeking their soul mates; from business
leaders looking to achieve their next level of financial or personal
success to artists seeking a more profound source of inspiration
for their work.

They are very different people enjoying the same wonderful
result—a much-needed reinvention that brought significant
physical, spiritual and financial rewards.

> It is our choices, and not our circumstances, luck,
> or relationships that define the course and quality
> of our lives, as well as our ultimate personal
> satisfaction and success.

MAKING POSITIVE CHOICES
The Secret Behind Personal Success

Most people don't realize the strength that lies in the Power of
Choice.

The Power to Reinvent our Lives is available to all of us by
making new choices at any given point and time.

Too many believe it's the other way around—that we are
always at the mercy of external forces.

This isn't to say that our environment or life circumstances
don't influence us; sometimes, we do need to re-assess our
choices, and alter the course of our direction.

We alter our choices based on a negative outcome that we can foresee, and we stick to our choices when we know that the outcome will be successful and positive for ourselves, and those around us.

For example, you may, as we did, have tickets to fly to Orlando, a famous tourist destination, only to find out there's a hurricane on the way there. You will inevitably change directions. You couldn't have anticipated this. Life throws curves at us all the time. Have you ever changed your plans because of circumstances you couldn't control? We all have had that experience. At that time, you look at your best choices and consider altering your plans.

Still, realize that the power of choice is always at work, and you are always making choices…even if they may be altered at times for circumstances beyond your control.

After all, none of us are perfect, neither are we asked to be. This imperfection, rather, is part of the design of our lives— because it conveys new meaning to our lives, even if it brings *pain* along with it.

And if you're wondering…

WHY DO WE EXPERIENCE PAIN?

Although, pleasure, nature, joy, adventure and love are some of my favorite teachers, I have learned that *pain is the greatest catalyst for our personal changes and growth.*

Many people get their biggest breakthroughs and make the most life-changing decisions from painful experiences, rather than from pleasurable moments.

The challenges you take on will always end up strengthening you, raising you up and not defeating you.

For me, one of the first profound examples of how pain triggers personal growth came back when I was getting my master's degree in Psychotherapy. During that time, I worked as an intern in an addiction facility and saw for myself that it was the pain of hitting rock bottom that often motivated addicts to finally break free of their self-destructive habits and begin to build a better life for themselves and their families.

These were people who destroyed their careers, their personal relationships, and their finances. They had nothing left and nobody left to blame except themselves. That in turn influenced them to finally, finally say, "I need help"—those three magical words that were necessary to begin their recovery and transform their lives.

That's what happened with the addicts I observed. Their pain brought about the powerful realization that they had to change their life choices and break their habits. They realized they got to make choices to either stay where they are or reach for a higher purpose.

What do I mean by that?

We are all addicted to something in some form or shape. And the reason *why* some addicts do what they do is pretty basic: Everything is geared towards getting more of their drug of choice and that keeps them where they are. However, when an addict breaks out of their vicious cycle and gets clear of their addictive habit, they are forced to confront who they really are and what they really want out of life. In this context, pain becomes a conduit for change.

> Pain is not the enemy; it is a motivating force for change.

See pain for the transformational catalyst it can be— and realize the choices it can bring into your life!

As the saying goes: Pain happens to all of us and we all have to deal with it but suffering is optional.

Seen in this way, pain is a signal that change needs to be made for any effective transformation to occur, and to move forward and not stay stuck in the past. Pain can be used to trigger change in yourself. It can serve to motivate others, it can be useful to relate to others, to identify with others, to share our own experiences of pain, hope, and victory, with others, letting them see that there is a reason for their pain, that it is not meaningless because no painful experience happens in vain.

The world is full of people who made the greatest difference, after being motivated by a personal, painful experience. Just think about someone you admire and the hurdles they went through, and I will have proven my point. Pain brings with it a choice of whether to endure it, change course, or to let it go. Ultimately, it makes you think about your 'why.'

OH ME, OH MY!
Checking Your Why, What, and Who?

1. **Why is it important for me to achieve my goals and Reinvent my life?**

2. **What new choices do I need to make to be prosperous from my decisions?**

3. **Who do I have to become in order to achieve what I want out of life?**

Asking yourself these questions will always bring profound answers that lead you to make more positive choices that fulfill your purpose and passion.

Next, let that 'Big Why' drive your decisions and your life and you will always have the energy to move forward. When passion and purpose fuel you, you don't count every hour in the day; instead, you make every hour count.

CHOOSING MEANINGFUL GOALS

When we choose to work towards a greater purpose, a cause, a mission larger than ourselves we tend to achieve more. With a greater purpose our inspiration grows, our consciousness transcends all boundaries and we become empowered to redesign a marvelous new world for ourselves and those around us, where our dormant qualities reawaken, and you will discover that *you are much more than you think you are.*

So, choose meaningful goals and activities to keep your passion alive. Look for a career, a hobby, or volunteer work that excites you and gives you a sense of purpose. Answering the question above will guide you towards your purpose.

**With purpose, you can use your
Gift of Choice to the fullest!**

The first step to harness your ***Power to Reinvent your Life***, or any aspect of it, is to determine why are you here, what you want in life, and who you want to be.

Reaching that kind of decision in your life will take time, as well as careful consideration. It will involve self-awareness, exploration, and motivate inspired action. You will need to set your priorities and determine the specific areas of your current life that require a makeover.

Through that process, you, too, can achieve what you need to move forward. When that happens, everything in your life will seem to magically fall into place and you'll be able to see, maybe for the first time ever, what you can do in spite or your circumstances, and what you need to change to fully enjoy the life you want to have.

> The choices we make will be the turning point in our lifetime of personal achievement...or not!

ALEXA'S STORY
(Case Study 1)

To understand how important choices are in identifying solutions to our situations, I'd like to share the story of Alexa, one of my seminar participants. Alexa lived for others more than she did for herself. Throughout her adult life, she failed to focus on her career. Instead, her efforts went into sustaining a series of dead-end relationships that didn't bring her happiness, most ending broken. That's because she didn't develop herself. Instead, she was consumed with making sure everyone else got the best impression of her, and also what they needed in their lives, while she remained stuck in the same place, year after year.

By the time I met Alexa, she was in her early forties, living a life that was defined by whoever was in her life at the time and not by her own needs, strengths, and abilities. Nothing she did was an actual reflection of what mattered to her—she didn't even *know* what mattered to her anymore. What she did know was that she was feeling the pain of wasting all those years on other people's dreams and not her own.

Alexa lacked the clarity to make good life choices. So I asked her, "What do you value in life? What do you want to have in your life that you're lacking now? What do you think could fill the emptiness inside?"

With those questions in mind, we identified what mattered to her and what she really wanted from her life. And what she desired more than anything else at this stage was to be in an unconditionally loving relationship and to have a fulfilling career where she could make a difference—the same things most of us want. But it was the first time Alexa felt comfortable admitting to those goals.

And that in turn brought her *to realize she could make positive choices and she, too, could harness The Power to Reinvent her Life.*

This was the beginning of her success. She changed how she approached relationships. She explored other careers and job opportunities in a way that she never had before. With new self-confidence and enthusiasm, she opened herself up to different possibilities and began to discover much more about who she was, learned how to love herself, which in turn empowered her, to make better choices to improve her life.

Six months later, after making all these changes within herself, Alexa met a marvelous, loving and caring man. A little later, she also found a new and more fulfilling career in the admissions section of a prominent college where she has the opportunity to encourage and help students to transition to their next level of education.

These things only happened because she was willing to reinvent herself following the steps and strategies proposed here. Following this system strengthened her to take action and take the necessary steps, for the first time in her life, which allowed her to pursue her own dreams and not someone else's. That in turn fired up the passion that motivated her to face those challenging goals and turn her life around.

THE FUTURE IS YOURS

A crucial takeaway from Alexa's story is this: **Every positive choice you make leads to a new pattern of reinvention**.

It was the first time Alexa heard it was okay to put herself first. This was like the first time someone starts jumping on a springboard; each time they bounce higher and higher. I could see the jump she made in her own life, and how she came out of her cocoon, knowing that for the first time she felt worthy and in control of making choices that improved her own life.

When you start making choices that empower you, your problems will seem to be further away and you'll be able to expand your options for reinventing your life and excel in finding solutions to realize your goals.

IT'S NEVER TOO LATE

The right choices make your life dreams possible, the kind of dreams that had been out of reach before.

Yet, you may be afraid to make those choices. You may feel the aspirations you once held for your future are now out of reach. You may even be thinking of giving up on them.

What you don't realize, however, is those aspirations can still be fulfilled. It's never too late!

THE PAST DOES NOT DEFINE YOUR FUTURE

Every choice you make in the present moment together with the energy you infuse to your actions on a moment-to-moment basis is what continues to define your future.

Still, many people find it difficult to move beyond the negative decisions they've made in the past and live in remorse. They continually blame themselves over and over for the failures they've endured, instead of focusing on what they need to do to turn their lives around.

If this is a challenge for you, or someone you know, it always helps to remember we're not alone.

You can also take comfort in these facts:

Every mistake is a learning lesson, and with the experience you've acquired in the past, you're now better equipped to use your Power of Choice for future goals; and in the same way your past experiences will help discern the exact kind of results you wish to achieve through your reinvention. You'll also be better equipped to help others in theirs.

Other people have forgiven themselves for poor decisions and come out winners. If they can do it, so can you.

Most of all, you must keep in mind that **the past has already been written—but the future is like a blank canvas, open wide, just for you**. By letting go of old patterns and harmful behaviors, transformation is now possible, and the future can be seen through a new lens. That shift in perception, however, requires being transparent and totally honest with yourself, even if it takes you out of your comfort zone. Only then, with a clear panoramic view, can you exert the Power of Choice in a meaningful and impactful manner.

Here's an unusual example of how letting go of the past reaped huge rewards. And it concerns a magazine, not a person!

As a lover of nature, one of my favorite magazines has always been *National Geographic*. In recent years, however, print publications have faced challenging times due to similar content being available on the Internet at no charge—and *National Geographic* was no exception.

In the early 2000s, the company began to lose money. There was so much value and goodwill in its brand, however, that CEO John Fahey wisely looked at ways to update its approach and delivery systems through modern media.

Today, *National Geographic* is far more than a magazine, it's now an entertaining and informative (not to mention profitable!) presence on TV and online. If Fahey had continued to limit it to what it had been in the past, however, the publication would have slowly spiraled into bankruptcy. Through the Power of Reinvention, however, he saved everything that was good about the brand while getting rid of what was dragging it down.

Like Fahey, you can define clearly what aspects of your life need reinvention and which you need to let go of. In this way, you too can take control of your future.

YOUR UNLIMITED POTENTIAL

Throughout my journey coaching, I've identified some core situations where reinvention becomes the key to jumpstarting our passion, purpose, happiness, and success. For example, in the area of personal relationships, I've had the privilege to work with couples that were on the brink of divorce. However, when both parties were willing to reinvent their relationship (and, at the same time, work on their own personal development), in almost every case they succeeded in saving their marriage. In our seminar settings, sometimes the healing happened instantly, whereas other times it took more time and effort. In all cases, however, when couples applied themselves to the areas that required improvement, they ended up reconnecting with each other and rekindling the initial passion and excitement that brought them together in the first place.

Of course, rocky relationships, losses, or changes aren't the only things that motivate reinvention. For example, your body and your self-image might not be in alignment. Your business or your career might need a shift in strategy. Or there may be a huge conflict between your actions and beliefs systems that continually make you insecure and question yourself. Whatever crisis point you might be facing, your potential for progress is unlimited if you open yourself up to using your Inner Forte™, the strength within you, to *Reinvent Your Life*.

FORWARD MOVEMENT IS POWER

There are some traditional beliefs that hold the notion that when you move things around in your home, or in life, you increase your luck. In other words, when you make new choices, like occupy a new living space, begin a new relationship, move to a new city, start a new job, or even shift your consciousness to a new point of view, you are creating the conditions for positive change. This belief is rooted in the fact that when you change something important in your life, it forces you to get out of your comfort zone and grow to fit your new situation.

I have the power to make positive choices

I am basically an optimist and whether it comes from the positive upbringing our parents provided for us, or from my innate nature, I too believe this to be true, that: *There is magic and power in movement and in making bold choices, especially* when those choices are made to pursue positive changes.

Every tiny movement you make to achieve your goals creates forward motion and it all counts. Just 1% small improvements made daily will add to your 100% potential. The Japanese know this phenomenon as "kaizen," that seemingly small insignificant change that keeps adding up and creates amazing results when done gradually, and consistently.

> When you keep putting one foot in front of the other, when you stay focused on what you want, Your success will inevitably find you.

When people keep doing the same thing over and over, and find themselves stuck in the same place, they end up in a rut and stagnate. In contrast, when you stir things up, you feel and look at things completely differently. You find out more about yourself and this new perspective in turn, brings you to a profound sense of clarity.

Yes, I'm saying change is necessary before you reach clarity. Changing the way you think, and overcoming your resistance to success, as well as changing your physical environment are important things to consider. Often times you know when you have to make a move, even if it doesn't seem completely logical or rational. Getting out of that rut can be incredibly beneficial, even if it just involves a temporary shift like taking a trip to somewhere you've never been before by bus, train, car, foot, plane, or boat — and even if you take that trip by yourself. My point is, leaving your comfort zone brings new insight and new attitudes.

There is magic in boldness. When you follow your heart and mind, you find your way to reinvention—and you'll lift yourself up to where you belong!

YOUR FIRST STEPS TOWARDS REINVENTION

Even successful people need Reinvention in their life to continue their success. Here's how we do it, and how you can Jumpstart your Process right now.

THE REINVENTION PUZZLE

Explore the different areas of your life, each working like a piece of a puzzle, and notice how you feel about each one to determine which piece of your puzzle needs your attention right now.

Rate each area on a scale from 1-10. Allow yourself to be totally honest and transparent in order to achieve clarity about the areas you feel you need and want to reinvent at this time of your life.

1. Health	1	2	3	4	5	6	7	8	9	10
2. Success/Wealth	1	2	3	4	5	6	7	8	9	10
3. Relationships	1	2	3	4	5	6	7	8	9	10
4. Family	1	2	3	4	5	6	7	8	9	10
5. Career/Business	1	2	3	4	5	6	7	8	9	10
6. Recreation	1	2	3	4	5	6	7	8	9	10
7. Spirituality	1	2	3	4	5	6	7	8	9	10

Following are some questions to help identify the work you need to do:

1. **Financial Freedom?**

   What is your attitude towards Success and Wealth? It may come as a surprise, but financial freedom has less to do with the amount in your bank account than your relationship with money. Those with a healthy relationship with money know that it is a tool rather than a means to happiness. It's never more important to them than the true joys of life.

2. **Healthy Relationships?**

   Relationships can be the biggest help to your reinvention, or the biggest obstacle. It can be difficult to admit, but often our circle of friends and acquaintances include toxic individuals.

   Remember that you have the power to choose who you allow into your life. If your "best self" wouldn't include certain people in your inner circle, it's time to begin easing yourself out of those specific relationships. Please keep in mind this does not mean that you avoid helping others who are in need of your knowledge or care; it does mean, however, that you take care of yourself first.

3. **Work and Life-balance?**

   Do you work so much that it takes its toll on your health and your relationships? Do you find yourself getting less and less enjoyment out of life? Identify ways you can shift that imbalance and make time for activities that bring you peace and happiness. We were not put on earth to mimic the hamster on a wheel, spinning around constantly and never truly enjoying the ride. **Remember, Happiness and Success are journeys, not destinations.**

4. **Good health?**

   Do you pay attention to what your body is trying to tell you? Or do you ignore those messages and continue unhealthy patterns?

If the latter is the case, how can you begin to make the kinds of choices that will leave you feeling stronger, more energetic and able to accomplish more?

5. Putting yourself first?

Many people in the most desperate need of reinvention consistently place their needs behind everyone else's. If that's the case with you, make your care and wellbeing a priority. Look for a sanctuary space where you can rest and reenergize, surrounded by things you find beautiful. Meditate there and get in touch with your inner self, so you can find the clarity and strength to move forward.

7 Strategies for Wielding Your Power of Choice

Here are a few excellent strategies to ensure you use your Power of Choice to Reinvent Your Life to the fullest extent:

1. **Love Yourself**

   Love, accept and approve of yourself exactly as you are right now and where you are in your life at this moment, and you will empower yourself.

   Here's why that love and approval is so important:

   When you allow yourself to love yourself unconditionally, with all your strengths and, yes, even your imperfections, your instinctive, ego mind is freed from any obstacles you might put in your own way. Instead, it feels the freedom to align with your dreams and collaborate with your reinvention plans. You also increase your self-confidence and feel self- assurance as you leap into action.

   And here's my favorite reason for wanting you to empower and love yourself: You no longer approach life as a victim awaiting defeat. Instead, you feel fun and fulfilled in your newfound power—and feel like the sky is the limit!

2. **Approve of Yourself**

   You can live your life authentically, on your own terms, and avoid becoming preoccupied with the thoughts and opinions of others by reminding yourself that they're too worried wondering what *you think of them! Instead, move forward, confident that your intuition is leading you in the right direction.*

3. **Embrace the Bold and the New**

   Make bold moves by choosing new interests that match up with your most prominent goals and interests. For instance, you may keep trying to become a great tennis player—even though you're not good at it and don't even care about it that much. Why continue? You'll find the most potential for growth in areas where you show natural aptitude, as well as high interest. Think about what you're good at that you also really enjoy.

4. Be Assertive (and Act on It Too!)

When you feel strongly about something and fail to either express yourself or act in line with those feelings, you inevitably feel regret or even embarrassment. Why? Because your ego stings more when you hold back and don't live what you feel. It becomes harder and harder to forgive yourself each time you repress yourself.

> Get in the driver's seat now! Only you can empower yourself and take control of your life.

The trick to being assertive is doing it in the right way. Tune in, pay attention to your body's cues, listen to your deepest needs, make a decision to trust yourself, and then don't ignore it, instead, speak up and put your words into action.

5. Move Your Body—Get off the couch...

While meditation brings calmness and inner peace, the movement of your body brings power with it. Moving your body stimulates your mind.

The moment you begin to move your body, everything in you changes, endorphins begin to fill your brain and you see life in a different light.

Any physical activity is a great choice for the body and has become a popular way of caring for your physical health, as it helps stretch out muscles and ligaments, and tone the body. Physical stagnation leads to mental and emotional overload.

6. Utilize your Potential

Reinvention requires your all – so avoid the mistake of doing 'just enough.' Raise your standards and go above and beyond the minimum effort and be creative in how you do that. For example, if you need to exercise once a week to reach your weight loss goal, hit the gym, the park, or even home two times per week and then also perhaps add a dance class or something fun to your routine. Allow yourself to get the extra support you need to motivate yourself, tap into your highest potential in any given task, and your success is practically guaranteed.

7. Grow your Reinvention Gifts with Daily Gratitude

Gratitude increases the gifts you reap as you move along your reinvention path. To grow those gifts even more, be thankful not only for the progress you've made, but also the setbacks. Having a grateful attitude is important. It helps you stay humble, which, in turn, powers your ultimate transformation.

Wise choices create the vision of life ahead clearer. Ever wondered how to create a compelling vision?

CHAPTER 2

Focusing On Your Vision

"Vision is the key to fulfill the greater purpose of your life, acting like a compass, leading you in the right direction every step of the way."
Yvonne Dayan

It's essential to have a precise vision for what you want to bring into your life and to keep yourself laser-focused on that vision.

Imagine you are looking at the ideal picture of how you want to be at the end of your Reinvention journey. Can you picture the 'new you' in your mind?

If you can create a picture of where you want to go, with an objective mind, it's much easier to reach that special destination. With that in mind, ask yourself the following questions that will help point you in the right direction:

- What do you want your future to be like? Can you imagine it?
- What qualities would you like to acquire or improve on?
- How do you plan to reach those goals?

Your answers will go a long way towards designing the vision you will need, to get the most out of the new you.

WHAT YOU SEE, YOU CAN BECOME

Your vision of your future is the driving force for your reinvention, opening the path to self-realization and enabling you to reach new levels of empowerment and joy along the way.

Your vision will inspire you to continue working towards your new-set goals and stay focused. With that vision, new leadership traits will emerge and allow you to effectively clarify, articulate, and project exciting possibilities for your future—as well as enlist others to support you in your efforts! When you share your vision with those around you, they, too, might catch the excitement you're adding to your own daily life.

VISION AND PURPOSE

On the other hand, as the sages who composed the Bible tell us, "Where there is no vision, the people perish." (Proverbs 29:18) When you lack vision, you also lack direction and purpose, making it difficult to actualize your mission and the emerging of your authentic self.

That's why now is the time to lock in the vision of your

authentic self, to lead you where you want to go and who you want to be when you get there. With that vision, you can become the success you want to be and lead the way to creating your best life. And keep in mind there is nothing too small or too large to consider when formulating your vision. If it feels right to you, then it should be included.

Here are 5 powerful exercises that will enable you to sharpen your vision and achieve what you're truly after in your heart and soul:

1. **Imagine doing at least one thing you have always wanted to do.**

   Think about what has prevented you from reaching your goals and think about how to overcome whatever obstacles have been in your way. What steps could you begin to take to make your reinvention goals a reality?

2. **Envision yourself cultivating your Inner Forte the virtues and strengths within you that you may have been neglecting over the years.**

   These are positive attributes that attract you to others and that you feel you may possess, but for one reason or another, have never had the opportunity to develop properly. With your Inner Forte™ activated you can unlock your gifts and put them into action in your life.

3. **Picture what will bring you lasting joy.**

   Happiness does not need to be limited to a brief response or to a fleeting circumstance—it is possible to make it an integral part of your daily existence with this daily practice:

   Pause for a moment, then, breathe joy into your vision of the future, and exhale positive energy all around you. Take 2 or 3 more breaths, concentrating only on things that trigger good feelings, and from that feeling state, determine what elements you want that will promote contentment and lasting fulfillment to your journey of reinvention. Keep in mind that happiness is not freedom from the chaos; rather, it is finding joy amidst the chaos.

4. Be very specific.

Vagueness and a lack of definition in your vision will leave you confused and lost when trying to reach your destination. So be as descriptive as possible (while still leaving yourself some flexibility and "wriggle room") when it comes to who you want to be and where you want to go.

5. Open yourself up to endless possibilities.

Most people fail to grow and develop simply because they get blocked by self-inflicted limitations. Avoid the trap of falling back into those limitations. Instead, free yourself from them, and focus on what's possible for you in order to access your Inner Forte, your true potential and focus on your most prized and authentic aspirations.

CREATE A COMPELLING VISION

Vision unlocks incredible motivation. With your vision in place, you may discover you have ambition and drive unknown to you previously. That is the spirit of the Real You coming to the forefront leading the way, emerging from the depths of your soul, looking to propel you onward with your transformation.

When your vision can hold a future that fills you with a sense of hope, meaning and fulfillment, that, in turn, creates the fire that fuels your passion to achieve that desired purpose, no matter what age you are, how others criticize you, how your children react to you, who abandoned you, what situation you find yourself in, or what cards life has dealt you in the past.

You can always reinvent your life anytime and anywhere when you have a compelling vision in place.

A compelling vision is further empowered by your most cherished values.

Different people, of course, have different values. Some value happiness above other things, others value love, altruism, justice, and/or beauty. Have you ever stopped to think... what do you value?

I am one of those people who has beauty as one of their core values. But my definition of beauty isn't the usual one, which only considers outside appearances. No, the beauty I value comes from an inner state of harmony and peace, creating an energy bursting from within that creates an exquisite balance of strength and softness, action and stillness, courage and grace, weaving them together, and triggering the same beauty in those who are fascinated by it.

Someone whose story triggered my curiosity began in a place of overwhelming physical beauty, and then found a way to transition to the kind of beauty I'm talking about. She redefined her vision through her core values.

One door may need to close before many other more important ones will open for you

The person I'm talking about is Frederique van der Wal of Victoria's Secret fame. When her modeling career came to an end, she reinvented herself by embarking on a new vocation in creating beauty through flowers.

As the founder of Frederique's Choice, she established herself as a capable florist and excellent businesswoman. She showed herself to be more than a pretty face as she transitioned from modeling to entrepreneurship and found business success, through a meaningful career that delights and inspires all of us.

The life of a former model has many, many pitfalls—Frederique van der Wal escaped all of them through a profound reinvention that was a true blessing.

There are many lessons you can take from her story, but here's mine: *"If you ever find yourself at the end of a career, at the end of a relationship, at the end of your inspiration, at the end of your parenting days, at the end of any major phase, it just might be a blessing in disguise—because it frees you for true reinvention, which allows you to discover a new facet of yourself, and propels you towards your next glorious mission in life!"*

SEEING PAST YOUR ROADBLOCKS

Often life reinvention gets sidetracked and postponed for many reasons. People feel blocked; they think they're incapable of instigating the change they need to make, the progress they desire, or they may lack a proven reinvention system that can do what we've been discussing in this chapter—creating a compelling vision for themselves and actually following through to finally seeing the success they want to achieve.

When people don't feel inspired, they can't picture themselves moving forward. They feel stuck and that negative thinking keeps them where they are.

If this sounds familiar, then the way to progress, to spark motivation and diligently expand your vision beyond your current limited horizon, is to open up your vision to include others in it; to serve others around you; to entertain causes that are bigger than you, to love and serve others unconditionally, and entertain a higher level where you can take your life to. When you can raise your own standards and expectations for your own success, that success has no option but to come meet you on your terms!

They call those special few who create enormous change visionaries for a reason. I'm talking about legendary people like Einstein, Gandhi, and Madame Curie, who were able to 'see' reinventing not only for themselves, but for the world around them, and as a result made amazing things happen!

What they did you can do, or not... but maybe! The point is, if you dare to imagine it, you will feel emboldened to achieve it. And that vision will give you the key in terms of discerning what direction you must take to achieve your desired outcome. Temptations that distract or detract from reaching your goals will be easier to shrug off, no matter how attractive they may seem.

It's been said that: What you see in your mind, you will hold in your hand.

The meaning of that wise statement is that if we want to attract certain positives in our life—new and exciting people, more favorable circumstances, more money, a better career, a richer personal life and a more successful professional life—we must first be able to envision them being possible.

That process begins by using your vision and engaging your imagination.

ENGAGING YOUR IMAGINATION

Engaging our imagination is a powerful way of telling The Universe exactly what it is that you want to manifest—and is an essential ingredient in developing a vibrant, powerful, and unified vision. This is your next step in developing that vision.

Imagination is actually the gateway to a better reality because it allows us to form a desired mental image not available through the five senses. In Einstein's words, "it is the preview of life's coming attractions."

Imagination, however, is frequently written off as mere daydreaming, an activity most of us have been discouraged from since we were children. Whether in school, at work, or even in social settings, if we stare off into the distance entertaining some incredible possibility, we are told to return to reality.

When I was a kid I use to get lost in dream-land and I heard that phrase many times, in different intonations, and depending *who* said it, I knew if I was in trouble or not. One day my dad lovingly said to me, "Yvonne, come back to reality, the world needs you here. One day you'll be taking people there. But for now I want you here and not out there." At the time, I did not know what he meant.

The truth is, imagination is the motor behind your vision, which is why it's good to give it a regular workout. How else can you fine-tune your imaginative skills?

Through imagination, you can use visual imagery to manifest your desired future. This is a process that does go beyond daydreaming. Instead, you want to use your imagination in a targeted way. **You want to daydream with a purpose in mind**, a purpose we believe in that drives us on.

> To develop a concise vision, your imagination must have a strong, clear and consistent intention.

Once you see that image, and feel the emotions inherent in it, you then need to visualize it as happening NOW, and not in the future. This way, you are aligning your vision with the Universe, and rather than sending mixed messages, you are now sending clear signals of what you want to manifest in your life.

STAY IN CONTROL!

When you are actively engaging your imagination, you are in control. You are consciously directing your thoughts towards a specific purpose and developing your vision. And that's all to the good.

But danger can come when you are going through your day-to-day life—and other images interrupt and disrupt your vision.

What most people don't realize is that they are already using the art of visualization and the power of manifestation, whether they are aware of it or not. Unfortunately, many people are actually visualizing the things that they *don't* want, the people they *don't* want to attract, and the events they *don't* want to occur.

When you're in a bad or fearful mood, you think about the worst that can happen. And that's just as powerful as thinking about the best! The Universal Force does not differentiate between what you want and don't want—instead, it responds to whatever powerful mental images you generate and the strong emotions that are attached to them. In turn, those images get manifested into realities. That may be why some people find that they always end up in the wrong types of relationships, take on the wrong type of work or never seem to make any financial progress.

This Universal Intelligence sees what you see. So, you must be decisive and selective!

WHAT ARE YOU LOOKING AT?

When I say you must be selective, I'm not just talking about what you put into your imagination. I'm also talking about what you put in your house and in your office, and in your environment.

What do I mean by that? Everything you see feeds your imagination. If you surround yourself with paintings, sculptures and pictures that are disturbing, then, you will feel disturbed. If you constantly watch horror movies, you may feel too much fear. If you read or watch too much bad news, it can raise your anxiety level and disrupt your peace of mind and quality of life.

What you need to understand to put these ideas to work in your life is that your subconscious mind is always alive, watching, listening, and reacting to whatever you're encountering on a conscious level. You should use that fact to your advantage—*for you have the power to choose and select what you expose your subconscious mind to, which, in turn, will impact the vision you are setting for your reinvention.*

With that in mind, use all the visuals that surround you to stimulate and support your vision, not undermine it. Think about the commercials with which the advertising agencies bombard our unconscious mind. They're filled with beautiful images to promote their clients' benefits. Do as they do. Use your power to choose what you see and encourage your ideal vision.

For example, if you want to create a new vision to reinvent relationships, and go from singlehood to marriage, then add pictures of couples' images that reflect love, caring, togetherness, and passion.

During my last reinvention course, I recommended to one of our participants who had been single and had shared that she was now ready to find her soul mate, to change the painting of that solitary figure that she had up on her wall for years and switch it out with one of a loving couple having the romance of their lives.

If you want to reinvent your financial situation or career, do the same. Add pictures, paintings and graphics in your house, office, and on your computer screen that reflect abundance, wealth that build enthusiasm and draw prosperity your way.

Another example is Nadia, a course attendee, who after learning this strategy was motivated to take action, went home and glued her "Reinvention Map" with a (fake) $100,000-dollar bill to the ceiling of her bedroom, straight above her bed, so that when she opened her eyes in the morning, it would remind herself to visualize abundant wealth coming into her life. After practicing visualizations exercises diligently for about 60 days, she noticed an increase of happy clients; and soon after she received an award for becoming the top seller in her real estate office.

Whatever you want, whatever you direct your vision to reflect, make sure it is represented in what you see in your surroundings. The magic happens once you synchronize the conscious and the unconscious mind, because these two parts of the Self share the same vision and the same powerful emotions.

7 Strategies for Focusing and Jumpstarting Your Vision

Take the following Action Steps to increase your attraction power through your vision.

Action Step #1: Identify Exactly What You Want

First, create a vision of exactly where you are today and where you want to be in the future.

Action Step #2: Align Your Actions with your Desires

Make sure that your vision, emotions and actions are aligned with what you want and need in order to make your life successful.

Action Step #3: Add Your Emotions to your Vision

In order to be effective, you just need to add your feelings to what you envision.

Action Step #4: Believe In What You Envision

When you are engaged in your vision, it is important that you truly release doubt and believe that what you are seeing in your mind will actually occur in your life.

Action Step #5: Trust Your Visualization

Even if you don't see what you envision becoming a reality right away, trust yourself that success is on its way! And affirm: "My best is coming to me NOW!" Once a day visualize and enjoy the outcome of your reinvention as if it has already happened.

Action Step #6: Release Worry, Fear and Control

Caution: This type of negative emotion contradicts the powerfully positive visualization that you are already engaging in.

Action Step #7: Practice Your Visualization Daily

Practice all the above steps consistently so that the force of the Universe will fulfill your dreams and visions and help you obtain the successful and joyous future you desire!

By staying consistent in your visualization and following the positive ideas and exercises of this chapter, you will be amazed at what you will achieve!

Now with our vision in place, let's take our next step and find out how we can transform our Mindset!

Control what you see and you begin to intentionally and deliberately bring into your life that which you truly desire.

CHAPTER 3

Transforming Your Mindset

"Shift your mind to believe and you will then achieve."
Yvonne Dayan

You may be much smarter than you think!

Through research, scientists at the Salk Institute discovered that the human brain's computing power is ten times greater than previously thought.

The new data suggests that you have the ability to process information as fast as the newest supercomputers and the capacity to store as much information as you can find on the entire World Wide Web right between your ears! With that kind of impressive mental capability, it's time to believe in yourself and in your capacity to expand your mind to its ultimate potential for success.

REPLACING LIMITING THINKING WITH LIMITLESS POSSIBILITIES

For reinvention to occur, be successful and to reap its rewards, you need to cultivate an open mind conducive to the kind of change you want to bring into your life.

That requires a 'mind makeover,' where *limiting thinking is replaced with limitless possibilities*. Likewise, obsolete beliefs that have been holding you back need to be switched out with actualized ones that serve to thrust you forward towards your higher purpose.

I have watched otherwise capable, smart, and qualified people remain stuck in their lives—and it wasn't necessarily because of any negative external circumstance. No, even though they had what it took to go further in life, they were trapped by their own outdated thought patterns. These thoughts skipped back and forth, in their minds like a broken record, convincing them that whatever they truly wanted to achieve simply couldn't be done.

As the saying goes, the mind is a terrible thing to waste!

The reason why people suffer is because of their constricted mindsets and their inability to accept to change. The opposite is also true; people progress because they allow for a new way of thinking, to take root in their minds.

Most people aren't even aware of how big a part their mindset plays in their lives. Often, that mindset is the biggest obstacle to transforming their lives in a way that matches the vision they have created for themselves and those they love. And I'm not just talking about big, epic goals like a fulfilling personal relationship or striking it rich.

For example, back in the day, when computers were somewhat new in the market place, I struggled with new technology. It would take me hours to figure out how to work new computer programs and even more time to use them efficiently. But a large part of that difficulty was my *attitude* towards that new technology. I viewed it as "too hard" and I made that judgment my truth. But you see, with that kind of judgment, I ended up losing time, resources, performance, and financial growth.

It's not the events, situation, people, politics, finances, or even our past that stops us from Reinventing ourselves into the highest vision we hold for ourselves, for our families and for our world. It is rather the way we think about those situations, people and events, the thing with the power to stop us.

Once I realized what I could gain through changing my outlook to a new mental approach, I decided to reboot my attitude and embrace the new technology. By changing my thinking, I could join the natural progression of the future of human evolution. So, I took it a step forward and created new positive beliefs that helped me realize new avenues to achieve what I wanted. Here are a few that you can adopt:

- It's easy for me to learn new and exciting technology programs and use them to grow my business!
- I love the tremendous advantages technology provides me!
- Technology is my friend; it helps me accomplish my desired goals quicker and better.

- I enjoy growing, evolving, and renewing my mind with the new advancements in technology!

Now, all of the above points are true. So why not embrace the truth? Why not make my life easier by reminding myself of them every time I face a new technological challenge?

In other words—**why limit myself with negative energy?**

RE-ENGAGE YOUR MIND
TO ACHIEVE YOUR VISION

In the previous chapter, I talked about the importance of step 2, having a compelling vision to guide us towards a successful reinvention. Once you have that vision in place, then you must bring your mindset to align with your vision in Step 3. Asking yourself these questions will help you achieve that alignment:

- Does the idea of your future motivate you?
- Does it excite you?
- What type of thoughts does it provoke in your mind?
- Are your actions moving you forward or holding you back?

This is a crucial crossroads in your success. If your mind cannot accept the vision of your reinvention, then it may actually sabotage your actions (just as my fear of technology sabotaged my efforts with computers).

That's why it's important to understand this principle: **"If you can envision it, then you have what it takes to achieve it."**

Here's how it works: New ideals and dreams are often placed strategically in our consciousness in order to awaken us and prompt us to move beyond what is known to us and move us into our highest potential. These ideals are an integral part of who we are. Sometimes we find resistance from our ego, which holds us back because it prefers to stay in its comfort zone, rather than boldly step into the unknown.

> ***Ultimately our ways of thinking***
> ***determine our successes or failures.***

As the saying goes, old habits die hard.

Often, I meet with people who think that what they have envisioned is not possible for them. My response?

"If you hold a strong desire in your heart, it is because you have the capacity to fulfill it." And I also advise them, as I now advise you, to own your *Power to Reinvent your Life* by adopting positive beliefs and declaring them your own.

Pause for a moment and declare it right now!

> ***"I can envision it, and I can achieve it."***

Consider the bumblebee. With its fuzzy round body and slight wingspan, this natural marvel should not be able to fly. However, the bumblebee only knows what it must do. It must gather pollen for nourishment, it must bring it back to its queen, and it must build a home with the other bees in its hive. With this knowledge, the intrepid bumblebee, ignorant of the laws of aerodynamics, lifts his round body into the air and confidently flies on his way, accomplishing what he must.

You, too, know what you must do. You will find it in your vision. And when your mindset embraces this vision, you empower yourself to achieve what may have seemed impossible to you.

Your Reinvention is not merely a transformation of body and physical aspects of your life; it's also a re-engagement of the mind and a renewal of soul. The key to realizing your ideals isn't in judging it to be true or false—after all, it hasn't appeared yet in tangible form, it can't be judged by those standards. No, the key lies in how you interpret your vision while on your journey.

It is within your ability and power to create the positive results you desire.

> ## A positive mental attitude will attract results that reflect your deepest desires.

THE SCIENCE BEHIND REINVENTION

One groundbreaking psychological study published by researcher Barbara Frederickson clearly exhibits the importance of positive thinking in opening the mind to possibilities.

In her research, Frederickson separated people into five groups. Groups 1 and 2 were shown images intended to create feelings of joy and contentment. Group 3 was the control group and viewed neutral, non-emotive pictures. Finally, Groups 4 and 5 were shown images intended to cause fear and anger.

After viewing their respective images, each group was given a sheet of paper with 20 lines and the prompt, "I would like to…" printed upon it. Interestingly, the negative image groups wrote the fewest responses, while the positive image groups wrote the most responses, beating both neutral and negative image groups alike.

Frederick discovered that negative thinking acts as a trap for your mind. It limits your ability to see options available to you or possible positive outcomes. Your brain essentially closes off entirely, and only focuses on the negatives.

On the other hand, positive thinking opens the mind, allows ideas to flourish, and enhances your ability to see possibilities that negativity may block out.

HOW THOUGHTS CREATE NEW REALITIES
My "Inner Forte 6-Point Formula"

The creative thought process of your mind allows you to have critical thinking and overcome obstacles in your life, therefore propelling you in your life reinvention. Below is a graphic that comes from my Inner Forte seminars/book, and that I'd like to introduce, which illustrates this process and features a phenomenon I call "The Wheel of The Creative Process (TCP).

Here's how this TCP "Wheel" works:

- Your beliefs create your thoughts.
- Your thoughts inspire your emotions.
- Your emotions motivate your actions.
- Your actions breed a specific set of results.

Here are some important aspects of this TCP wheel that I need to explain in greater detail. With the Inner Forte 6-Point Formula, you'll understand how to use this TCP wheel to your advantage and reframe your own beliefs to serve your vision and move it forward to create a successful reinvention plan.

43

THOUGHTS ARE NOT FACTS

First, remember that thoughts are not reality. If you take your negative thoughts at face value as 'the truth,' you will sabotage your own efforts. Keep in mind that your thoughts are just that—THOUGHTS—that can be changed and transformed to provide motivation and positive support.

1. Identify Limiting Beliefs

Look for every negative belief that does not serve you and does not reflect reality, keeping in mind these truths:

We all have the ability to identify and turn around those limiting beliefs.

Be aware of when these negative beliefs sneak into your conscious mind and prevent you from becoming your best self and living a full, satisfactory life.

2. Understand the Influence of Beliefs

Look back on negative patterns in your life to understand how your limited beliefs may have created these patterns.

Analyze the consequences of those beliefs and how they affected your actions (or even your inaction). By understanding the full effect of these negative beliefs, you will be motivated to let them go sooner rather than later.

Remember my experience with technology? Only when I realized how certain beliefs were having a negative impact on my business did I become motivated to change them!

3. Acquire Empowering Beliefs

Turn those negative beliefs upside down and consider what you ought to believe instead. Create empowering ones that will inspire positive action.

Say, for instance, that you or someone you know has the negative belief, 'it's too late to change.' This could be for a myriad of reasons. I've heard in my seminar people saying that they can't change because they are too old, or too set in their ways; others simply said they've tried too many times and just could not make it happen. But you defeat yourself with those negative ideas that limit your capabilities and undermine your efforts for positive change when the truth, is you can make a difference in your life, and the life of those you love.

Demanding too much of ourselves, putting rigid deadlines, comparing ourselves with others, means neglecting to relish every amazing step, with its joys and its challenges, its synchronicities and unexpected gifts as they naturally unfold along every Reinvention path.

A great way to upend these limiting beliefs is to question them, and ultimately change your focus. Because the reality is, every day is fresh, and we have access to a fresh beginning to reinvent ourselves anew.

I always like to remember that:

New possibilities bloom with each day!

And...

every day of our lives we can live with Joy, knowing that change is available in every present moment!

Entertaining thoughts like these is what motivate us into taking consistent baby steps in the direction of our dreams and is how we achieve our goals with greater joy.

Always look to turn a negative situation into a positive solution. This will open up new possibilities to jumpstart the areas where you are lacking, and also insure that you pick and fulfill the right goals to reinvent your life.

4. Think, Feel, and Act Differently

Use your reframed beliefs to transform yourself intellectually, emotionally, and spiritually. Be very specific about the change you want to see in yourself.

For me, I tackled new computer applications with my reframed belief system—and ended up loving the way I was now able to work with technology. It made my life easier and I experienced a lot of joy making that decision.

5. Persist

Finally, remember that it will take persistence to work through your own personal Wheel of Creative Process. It will take a lot of repetition and some time to replace your limiting beliefs with ones that serve you better. So, continually practice this 6-point Forte formula to fine-tune your attitude and make it work in your favor. Remember this: Bad attitude gives you no altitude!

Putting your Inner Forte TCP Wheel to work in such a positive way is an incredibly important part of your transformation. Your desires begin, of course, in your imagination; by using your creative process in a proactive way, you can create the kinds of empowering thoughts and beliefs that will allow you to transform these desires into reality. This in turn will give you more confidence and strength moving forward as you tackle your next level of reinvention!

> Every thought is like a seed—but that seed can only grow strong if your mind provides the right fertile ground for growth.

THE POWER OF ICA

Let's go into more detail about creating the right mental conditions for Reinvention.

Each successful Reinvention is born from the seeds of beliefs, thoughts, emotions, and actions. Of course, the seeds are not enough—they must be 'fed' the right ingredients in order to sprout into large healthy 'plants.'

How do we create the right conditions for these seeds to grow and thrive? I've created a mnemonic device called "ICA" to make it really simple. We feed them with:

- *INTENTION*
- *CHOICE*
- *ALIGNMENT*

These are the three ingredients that you need in your life to empower you to start going in a new and exciting direction. Let's take a closer look at these ingredients and see how we can use them to jumpstart our life Reinvention process:

1. **Intention**

   We are the one who gives meaning to our thoughts. If your intent is to progress in your life, then stay focused on that purpose, and infuse your thoughts with the energy that will carry that intent forward. On the other hand, if you keep changing directions and telling yourself that you're not very creative, you will find yourself shutting down opportunities to create change in your life. Intent is all-important in your mindset.

2. **Choice**

   Do you move forward or retreat? Do you expand your mindset or limit it? The answers can be found in the mental choices you make. You need to engage in thoughts that promote your intentions. The right choices create positive impact and increase momentum towards your reinvention. Choices made from fear or anxiety generally will limit you and hold you back. The choice of what to think is yours and yours alone, so use it well! Take something fun and exciting, like dancing. There are those who believe they will never be good at it and will never try. Then there are those who don't know…and keep dancing until they find out. Which person enjoys life more as a result of their choices? Yes, the one who is willing to explore and discover what they are capable of. So, before you surrender, try.

3. Alignment

When you are truly aligned with your words, dreams, and thoughts you easily harmonize and find acceptance with everything that's happening around you. Only then can you effortlessly align yourself with new opportunities and identify obstacles, clearly understanding how our mental attitudes best address both.

SELF-FULFILLING PROPHECIES

The dancing scenario I just described can easily be used to define the concept of self-fulfilling prophecies.

If someone who never danced before thinks they can't be a good dancer and doesn't try…well, then they can't be a good dancer.

However, if someone who thinks they can be a good dancer takes lessons and keeps at it…well, they probably *will* become a good dancer.

In both of the above cases, they fulfilled their own prophecies. But *only because of the opinion they held of themselves in the first place.*

Beliefs work in two ways. They can either activate the manifestation of life-giving forces or maintain the current negative and limited realities. This is why I said earlier how important it was to eliminate your own limiting beliefs—because, all too often, they mutate into negative self- fulfilling prophecies. It isn't because those ideas were true in the first place—it's because they prompted inaction or negative actions that caused the unwelcome result to come true.

This is just one example of how our beliefs cause certain results that have nothing to do with any reality except the one we hold in our minds. And that works both ways.

> The reality is whether you think you can or you think you can't... you're right!

If your mindset has a positive attitude towards achievement, you will go about tackling new challenges—and most times you will realize wonderful results from the willingness to take a chance.

HOLD FIRM TO YOUR BELIEFS
Announce the New You

To transform your new beliefs and bring them into reality stay focused, say them out loud, and that will in turn empower you!

Here's an example: Let's say you want to reinvent your career and jumpstart your way to a new job. Mentally put yourself in that position and affirm this aloud:

- "I (your name) am now in a fabulous job that I love that pays me abundantly."

Let's say the area of relationships is your focus for reinvention. Affirm this aloud:

- "I (your name) am now enjoying the most supportive, passionate and loving relationship of my dreams."

Perhaps you're looking to boost your self-confidence. Here is the belief you want to affirm:

- "I (your name) have *Absolute Self-Confidence™* in my own ability to reinvent a prosperous and fulfilling life for me."

And if it's a higher level of health and vitality you want to reach, affirm this:

- "I (your name) am now rejuvenating, healing, and replenishing all parts of my beloved body!"

When you affirm yourself in the new beliefs you're taking on, they take on more meaning and more substance. Watch those new beliefs gain strength!

CREATE YOUR NEW STORY

Along the same lines, begin to create a new narrative for who you are and what you're all about.

Everything you believe has also a great impact on how you feel about yourself and what you are willing to explore and experiment with. Those feelings are contained in our own self-narratives, in the stories we create internally to try and explain where we currently are in life and how we got there.

Usually, when we are after reinvention, there are at least some areas of our life where the story we tell ourselves isn't a great one. That's why, when you eliminate limiting beliefs, you need to also rewrite those stories that have a negative narrative to them.

As you replace those old beliefs with new empowered ones, write that new story in a way that reflects a new understanding of your past, and contains your authentic desires, your newfound passion, gratitude, and enthusiasm for the amazing opportunity to reinvent your life.

Bring to life a new story that motivates you and fills you up with the power to be the hero in your life. That story, in turn, will open up doors and allow you to reach your objectives.

THE MAGIC OF MEDITATION TO RELAX AND REINVENT YOUR SELF

Another wonderful tool in empowering your mind towards reinvention is the practice of meditation. Meditation allows us to regain control of our thoughts, as well as process the changes and choices involved as we move towards our success.

Meditation is especially important when we feel tired, tense, and stressed. That's when our minds are most vulnerable to being bombarded with all kinds of toxicity and negativity. We easily imagine the worst happening to us, we start doubting our choices, worrying, stressing ourselves and we end up taking on those bad projections as our probable outcomes. We lose control of our new beliefs and positive thoughts and slip back to old disturbing patterns.

When this happens, we need to take our control back. It's like being stuck out in the middle of the ocean, treading water and seeing huge waves about to crash down on you—and you have to somehow swim your way out to survive. Meditation gives you the strength to make that swim and reach the shore.

Meditation and hypnotherapy allow you to relax and jump-start your mind back in the right direction. It guides your body and mind to a peaceful state in which possibilities and positive options happily reassert themselves in your consciousness.

You'll feel more relaxed and hopeful, and that, in turn makes you more attractive to other people. People enjoy being around someone who seems positive, poised, serene, and relaxed. Who wouldn't?

Come to think of it, who wouldn't want to make meditation a regular part of their lifestyle? Once you learn, it's easy to do, and gives you the power to regulate any stress you're feeling in your life at the moment. And yet many people don't practice it.

There's a reason for that!

HOW TO OVERCOME YOUR NEGATIVE THOUGHTS WITH MEDITATION AND RELAXATION

Your ego wants you to believe there is not enough time to relax and enjoy your life. It convinces you it's a waste of time, because that's how it controls your life—by keeping you in a constant state of anxiety and rush. It's afraid and it makes you afraid! And that's when you really lose control of your mindset.

Please understand, it is you, and not your ego that controls your choices. When you are relaxed and balanced, the authentic part of you is in control of your choices. You can access the peace of mind to work through your reactions to stress. Meditation gives you the key to putting your authentic self back in charge in order to make complete relaxation possible.

When you notice your ego finding every excuse to avoid meditation and relaxation, it is within your power to reject that negative message.

Simply affirm to yourself, "I deserve to relax. It is **"ME TIME"** for replenishment and renewal. The more I renew and relax, the more energy I have to do the things I want to do."

Remind yourself what meditation does for you, no matter how crazy a day you might have— you'll be glad you did.

You just have to tell yourself that it's okay to take time out to renew your mind, body, and spirit on a daily basis.

MEDITATE AND RELAX

While meditation restores our inner balance, relaxes us, and allows us the ability to direct our mindset towards a more concise and positive direction, relaxation frees us from tension and anxiety, restoring in us a state of calm and peacefulness.

Besides meditation, you can also choose to relax on a regular basis. There are many ways to find relaxation, such as exercising our bodies, walking, enjoying time in nature. There are also other little things you can do to get into a relaxing mood, such as turning off the lights and using candles instead or turning on some soft music at a low volume and focusing on positive things. Whatever works for you, make sure it's a part of your schedule by telling yourself, and making it clear to others, that this is your time and your time alone.

In my work helping and teaching others how to relax, clients and students often shared with me how they struggled at night with sleep. They told me they would sleep for a bit but wake up after a couple of hours. It would take them time to get back to sleep and when they woke up the next day, they would often feel like they never went to bed at all!

That's why finding a way to calm yourself before bedtime can be so important.

It can be as simple as considering everything in life you feel grateful for or finding the positive in the day you've just lived. You can even consider the best way to enjoy the possibilities of the next day, so you can spend the night looking forward to what's going to happen.

At the same time, it is counter-productive to endlessly obsess about a rough day you might have just had or one that might be coming up. Instead, allow yourself to let go, and concentrate on how it may all work out for the best, whichever way it goes.

Being optimistic and positive will help you go to sleep with sweet relaxing dreams and bring you closer to your goals in joy and relaxation, rather than dwelling in anxiety and stress.

JUMPSTARTING YOUR MEDITATION PRACTICE

Reinventing your life requires reprogramming your belief system and motivating your subconscious mind to eliminate negative thoughts more quickly and more effectively: I myself share the views of many scientific studies that prove meditation is one of the best means to that end.

One rule I've repeated many times in my life, both to myself and to others, is this: *If you don't go within, you go without.* That's the reality.

The gifts of harmony, peace, serenity, balance, insight, and lasting joy all come from within. When we don't take the time to connect with what I call your Inner Forte, to access the wisdom and peace, and balance within us, then we try to meet our needs through other people, food, drugs, or whatever else we can find to give us that sense of 'okay-ness' and wholeness.

When we meditate, the gateway to the gifts of the spirit is opened. No matter how the ego wants to keep you from relaxing, you don't have to submit. Stay determined and proactively continue to build the habit of meditation and relaxation. You deserve (and need!) time out to relax and enjoy life.

If you are not used to having this kind of habit in place, you'll need to make sure it takes hold in your everyday life.

I can imagine that many of you reading this book aren't too sure how to go about meditating in an effective way.

That's why I've created a resource for you to use in order to help you begin meditating and reaping its relaxing rewards sooner rather than later. **A guided meditation audio CD titled** *"Reinvent & Jumpstart Your Life"* will help you relax, and specifically focus on reinventing your life to reap the rewards outlined in this book.

To find out how you can obtain a copy, please visit: **www. innerforte.com/meditations**

7 Strategies for Jumpstarting the Positive Transformation of Your Mind

1. Believe in Yourself

Believing in yourself is easier when you know that your potential is unlimited. Every human being has an inexhaustible supply of energy for transformation. When you reinvent your love life, your finances, your health, or any other aspect of your life, you draw from this unlimited *"Inner strength"*—and your belief in yourself becomes unshakable.

2. Remain Teachable

To continuously expand the scope of possibilities for improving your life, and use your brainpower to your advantage, remain teachable, and keep learning, even though you may no longer be in school as we know it. Read more. Sharpen your concentration abilities and let go of rigidity in your thinking so that you will hear the possibilities in everyone and everything.

Acknowledge that your best answers may come from the most unexpected places.

3. Unclutter Your Mind

Clear your mind so you can leave room for new ideas, new input and new growth. Be willing to trade bad habits for new ones. And get your unconscious mind on board.

4. The Best is Yet to Come!

Deepen your faith in yourself and strengthen the foundation of your new beliefs. Trust that good things are in store for you, that the best is yet to come! Believe in the Goodness of The Force that permeates the world, and in your innate capacity to tap into that goodness. Surround yourself with other achievers in the areas you want to excel in in order to boost and support your own winning mindset.

5. Develop a Giving Mindset

One amazing gift that comes with successful reinvention is that you suddenly experience immense gratitude for who you are and what you've accomplished. If you allow yourself to truly embrace this new harmonious state of thankfulness, you will develop a giving mindset.

Giving time, money, a smile, acknowledgement, compliments, love, a hug, happiness, and encouragement are powerful ways to develop an abundant and giving mindset. Most importantly, you will understand the eternal truth, "The more you give, the more you get back."

6. Refuse Personal Limitations Above and Beyond

Refuse to listen to the voices that tell you it's not possible. Don't believe those people that tell you, it can't be done. Instead, listen to those that encourage you, give you hope, enthusiasm, and convince you of your ability to believe in yourself. Know that thoughts are not reality. When you experience negative thoughts and immediately accept them as prophecy, you will stumble on your reinvention road.

So, keep in mind that your thoughts are just that – THOUGHTS. They can be changed and transformed just as you changed and transformed your outdated beliefs.

7. Promote a Positive Attitude

A positive attitude grows your magnetism, and draws the right people to your side, just as bees are drawn to honey.

A happy, joyous, and bright disposition goes a long way towards making your reinvention enjoyable and exciting. More than anything else in the world, a positive and cheerful attitude is your greatest asset to stay motivated while developing the abilities, expertise, and talents you'll need for transformation to occur.

Having a positive mindset will allow you to go your next step, trusting and knowing that you've got what it takes to successfully reinvent your life.

CHAPTER 4

Trusting Yourself
(You've Got What It Takes!)

"A bird sitting in a tree is not afraid of the branch breaking
because the trust is not in the branch, but in its own wings."
Unknown Source

Trusting yourself will boost your self-confidence, which is the key to jump-starting your life-reinvention process.

One of the most challenging yet crucial aspects of reinvention is discovering how to trust yourself and believe that... you've got what it takes to create the life you want. Even when you have already achieved some level of trusting yourself you'll have to admit there is always room to improve in this most important area of your life, and its companions: self-confidence, self-improvement, and self-love.

With self-confidence, you become empowered to make progress in your health, wealth, love, and all areas of life beyond your wildest expectations, because your faith in yourself grows to the point where you don't let anyone stop you from achieving your destiny.

Self-confidence allows you to trust yourself. Most often, we have been told to trust others, especially those in authority, but rarely have we been taught to trust our decisions and ourselves. Without trusting yourself, you only have doubt and insecurity as your counterparts.

Yes, you might still achieve a great deal. You might have a certain talent or influential connection to pave the way for you. But without a solid foundation of trusting yourself, those doubts can catch up with you and cause you to second-guess your best decisions, feel guilty, or procrastinate and keep you at a standstill, and in every case, cause you to delay your goals and dreams.

That's why trusting yourself is a necessity—and gaining it may be a challenging yet exciting aspect of your reinvention.

LOSING TRUST
Why We Lose Self-Trust in the First Place

Things happen to all of us. We all encounter negative situations, disappointments and losses. These can chip away at our confidence until doubt, fear, and anxiety become a prominent part of our mental habits. Self-judgment and criticism then deteriorate the way we perceive ourselves, until we begin to question our value as human beings.

That's when we lose self-confidence and the ego steps in, taking us on an emotional rollercoaster, convincing us that we are not enough, and worse of all, that we are not worthy. But that's just your ego's way of taking control, keeping you from being your best. What you need is to be more assertive and remove that mental junk from your mind, because the truth is…

Your worth should *never* be in question. **You are worthy just because you are.** *We are all born to be worthy—and nothing we do or don't do will change that immutable fact.*

As you continue on your journey to personal or work reinvention, you must believe that *change, transformation, progress, and evolution are possible*—and that your success will flow naturally when you start trusting the promptings of your Authentic Self and allow yourself to believe in all the possibilities in spite of past failures or fear; because… after all, you can ride on the wings of that indomitable spirit that lives within you.

Nature is a great teacher of trust. Think about the example in my opening quote: *A bird sitting on a tree is not afraid of the branch breaking because the trust is not in the branch, but in its own wings.*

Just in the same way, when the road to reinvention gets rocky, remember that your strength comes primarily from within you, and from those who love and support you, and who teach you to fly with your own wings.

So, dare to BELIEVE in your ability to navigate the path you are on. If you don't, no one else will. In the words of Mikhail Baryshnikov, one of the most amazing dancers of all time:

"I do not try to dance better than anyone else; I only try to dance better than myself."

Even when faced with failures, vulnerability and the unknown, move forward and put your faith and trust in yourself and in the Awesome Power of The Universe. Your efforts will always work out for the best; the answers you seek will come, and you will start figuring things out, with surprising results.

Now that you have created a positive mindset, empowering

you to move forward, continue by learning to engage both sides of your brain as a means to harness all your energies to continue reinventing your life to the fullest.

INTUITION
Left Versus Right Side of Brain Function

According to scientists, our brain has two separate hemispheres that work in very different ways. The left side of the-brain is more organized and systematic. The right side of the brain is more creative and intuitive.

My cousin is an engineer and a conceptual builder; that means he spends most of his working hours with the left side of his brain engaged. He can easily take the plans for a building, study them, make necessary changes, and create a practical blueprint for the structure that takes into account all necessary details.

Me? I'm the opposite. My work is well-organized, systematized, but not as tightly structured. My instinct is to draw pictures, get into the rhythm of things, and make choices that go beyond just being practical. They need to feel *right to* me.

Over the years, to gain balance, I've exercised the left side of my brain skills, while my cousin, on the other hand, worked more on the right side of his brain, because we both know we could use a little boost in those areas. We do this because we both know that integrating the qualities of both sides of our brains makes us more powerful more capable and whole.

And that in turn increases self-trust!

The left side of your brain predominantly controls your logical mind. During your reinvention, this part of your brain will help you analyze a situation, logically assess different possibilities and outcomes, and plan a rational course of action for your transformation. But that's not enough. Yes, it's crucial to be successful in your reinvention that you have a well-structured plan of action, but it can't do the job alone. That's because it's the right side of the brain where intuition and transformational magic becomes possible.

In the words of Henri Poincare, one of greatest scientific minds of the 19th century, *"It is through science that we prove, but through intuition that we discover."*

To take your reinvention to the next level, you must engage the right side of the brain functions, too. This half of your brain controls the abstract functions of your mind. Your intuition and trust centers are located in this part of your brain and give you almost-invisible guidance that serves as your internal compass to point you in the right directions.

When you are able to use the right side of the brain's intuitive abilities you increase your choices, and you tend to:

- Go with the positive flow more readily
- Act more inspired
- Expand your vision and see a bigger picture
- Be more creative and trust your feelings
- Get clear guidance on your journey
- Allow your intuition to lead
- Trust in your reinvention vision, even though it has not physically manifested yet.

THE MAGICAL COMBINATION

A balance of opposites is what creates harmony and makes us whole. The spiritual and the physical things of life are both important aspects of your reinvention journey. They each have something to contribute to empowering the new you.

Simply put, one force is the positive pole while the other is the negative pole. Consider the simple understanding of hot and cold, where the combination produces delicious warmth. Or the example of Stillness and movement, where one contemplates possibilities while the other one leaps into action. The two of them complement each other and work hand in hand to produce positive energy!

When these two powerful opposing players—the right and left sides of the brain—combine, they also bring together the best virtues of the heart and mind, together creating a rock-solid connection that aligns them both in your efforts. That allows us to become the recipients of the rare 'gift of wisdom' that directs us from the inside.

> No matter what adverse situation we may face in life, the important thing is to remain positive and trust our responses!

Consequently, the right side of the brain will intuitively guide you to protect you from dangers and sagely indicate which path to take at every juncture of your reinvention. While at the same time, your left side of the brain will take care to translate this sometimes-abstract wisdom into a reality that you can deal with on a practical level.

Without this deep dual connection, the ego can easily get in the way of your reinvention plans—because it, too, often uses doubt and fear in a mistaken effort to protect itself from any type of growth. It may even block you from doing things that will end up bringing you lasting joy.

By fine-tuning both sides of the brain, as explained, you

activate your Inner Forte, which will allow the underlying truth of every situation to become clearer to you. You will understand what you are really capable of achieving as it directs you towards your best choices, filling you with the conviction that you have within you what it takes to overcome challenges and move closer to your true destiny.

TRUST IN YOU ABOVE EVERYONE ELSE

Of course, challenges or crisis points during reinvention are only natural, *as each point of crisis hides within it a gift for you!*

To get to the gift though, it's necessary that you trust. Trust the process, trust the journey, trust others that The Universe puts on your path for them to help you, and for you to help them, and above all, trust yourself, knowing that you got **The Power to Reinvent your Life**!

Interestingly, the word *crisis* in Chinese is composed of two characters, respectively meaning *danger* and *opportunity*.

When you find yourself at a difficult crossroad, going through a crisis, this is precisely the time to love, nurture, support, and, most of all, trust in yourself, even if the outcome of the situation is unknown to you. This is part of the mystery of life.

Using the left side of the brain's analytical abilities to plan and discern, the path to follow is important, and just as essential is to understand that not every detail needs to be overanalyzed and bogged down with endless explanations, overthinking and logic. Amazing things can happen when you simply LET GO and let your inner compass steer your course.

Faith and trust, on the other hand, are intuitive functions. This is where magic happens in your life. This is the realm of the impossible becoming possible, the realm of manifesting effortlessly everything about you that you want to reinvent.

Have you ever had to make a decision and felt that you needed the advice of everyone around you in order to make the 'right choice'?

Imagine how wonderful it would be not to have to be asking everybody around you what you should or shouldn't do every time you face a challenge or a difficult choice…then trying to sort out all the advice and make sense of it.

That's when learning to trust yourself becomes crucial. No one knows your circumstances like you. No one knows YOU like you. You are the one who is best equipped to make your choices!

You have probably had strong hunches as to what you should do in a challenging situation. But you may have instantly dismissed them, thinking that they are somehow based in fantasy, not fact. They're not. They are part of your guidance system for reinventing your life. Of course, you must listen to the guidance and then assess its validity.

The next time you need guidance, simply practice listening and trusting your intuition and yourself. Then observe how your faith bolsters the inner wisdom that guides you and empowers your heart to direct your path towards your destination.

CONNECTING TO YOUR INTUITION

If you find it difficult to exercise your abstract-brain abilities and trust your intuitive hunches, here are some simple yet powerful ideas that will support you in doing just that:

- **Start small**

  Listen to music, dance, draw a picture, take a walk in a new direction, make up a song and sing it aloud—any small, unplanned burst of spontaneous creativity enhances your intuition.

- **Don't overthink it, just do it**

  When faced with a choice, your intuition may pull you in one direction, so don't dismiss it, listen to it. Then decide to follow it… or not. Intuition is deeply embedded in the right side of your brain and is almost always trustworthy.

- **Go with the flow.**

  Abandon your usual activities for a day, a week or a weekend. Go wherever chance takes you, move outside your comfort zone, and limit your rational response. Spontaneity comes from the right side of your brain and often results in examples of real truth your intuition automatically understands.

TRUST IN YOUR DREAMS, TRUST IN YOURSELF

In your daily life, you often feel the desires for those things you want to attain for yourself. This longing is generated by your intuitive mind.

> Self-trust is the secret ingredient to reinventing your relationships and jumpstarting a new life.

Once you can access that intuition, once you learn to trust those messages, then it's easier to trust in your dreams, especially when they incessantly call you over the years. You may have stopped listening to them, but they will always be with you, patiently waiting for you to respond to them and help actualize and materialize them.

These dreams are specifically given to you because of who you were made to be. They are yours, not anyone else's, and you have them because you were given the capability to achieve them. Trust that you have what it takes to bring your dreams to life!

Your level of success in reinventing your life is a direct result of how positive you are about yourself and how you feel about your efforts. The more you trust yourself, the more love, passion, success, and magnetism you will be infusing into every dream you have for all the areas of life you wish to transform.

With that in mind, just imagine how having Absolute Self-Confidence in yourself and your dreams could add enthusiasm and enjoyment to your reinvention.

Imagine how amazing your career or business could be. Think about how much improved your personal relationships could become. And consider how abundant and fulfilling your life journey would be, if you have the highest level of trust in who you are and what you can do.

And just imagine what you could have already done with your life had you trusted yourself more at an earlier age! How many opportunities have you missed—just because you didn't believe enough in yourself?

Everyone has their own story of how their lack of self-esteem hurt them in one area or another in the past. It causes some major regrets, because there is a cost to lacking self-trust. Whether it's in accomplishments that were never attained or desirable relationships that never came to be, we often hold back due to a lack of confidence in our personalities, our capabilities, and our attractiveness.

I know this since, sadly, I've seen so much talent, and wisdom, and opportunity wasted, or delayed, not for lack of desire or even drive, but because of the one crucial attribute that was missing from their lives: Faith in themselves. As I shared earlier, I was once there myself. That's why this is such a dear subject for me, and why I am a firm believer that for any reinvention journey to be successful, developing trust in yourself and having absolute faith in The Power of the Universe is key, no matter what has impacted your life.

Remember, you are not defined by what's happened in the past, because transformation is possible! You are defined for who you are becoming in the now!

So, don't look backward. Stay focused on where you are going and, just as importantly, trusting yourself will help create the best possible results! The past is just a reference point for your journey and was never intended to be your ultimate direction. Boosting your self-esteem will help you carve out a new path to your ideal success.

RITA'S SELF-TRUST CHANGED EVERYTHING
(Case Study 2)

It's not always easy to overcome low self-esteem and replace it with a high level of self-trust. But don't feel discouraged in that effort— because, as you'll see in Rita's story, when you succeed in it, it will ultimately encourage you to find more life satisfaction in everything you do.

Next, the case study that proves my point:

Rita, one of my course participants, came very confused, filled with worry and despair. During the course she noticed that she attracted the same type of wrong business partners over and over again. The first one stole money from her, the second one took advantage of her and did not give back in the same measure. She discovered that she kept attracting these people partly because she had a very low self-image that attracted others who knew they could easily get her to accept whatever they told her.

The same thing happened in her personal relationships. Because she always felt she was not good enough, she was willing to accept a lot just to maintain relationships of any kind. She didn't feel strong enough to assert herself, so, again, others preyed upon her. Without self-esteem she was simply too weak to say no when she needed to.

It was only after she started trusting in herself that this unequal state of affairs began to rebalance itself. She found herself strengthening her approach to others and not allowing them to take advantage of her. She found the courage to step out of her comfort zone and take the risks that would finally move her in the direction of achieving the goals she so desperately desired, as she finally felt comfortable enough to interact with people that honored and respected her.

These amazing results only came after she integrated 7 new habits that helped her create the foundation for this change.

I'm going to introduce my 7 Inner Forte Habits for Reinventing and Reigniting Your Life in *The Strategy* section of this chapter.

Adopt them and you will feel compelled to pull away from old and outdated self-perceptions, roles, habits, and comfort zones that may have blocked your life progress. As you make these new habits your own, your old self-defeating ones will fade away.

As you follow these habits, you'll find yourself gaining confidence in yourself until you can truly say, *"I trust myself—I have what it takes!"*

Next is another unusual example of how persistence and belief in reinvention reaped huge benefits. And it concerns the movie industry!

Most of you reading this book have heard of George Lucas, mostly because he created one of the most successful and beloved film series of all times, *Star Wars.*

And yet, he barely got the first movie off the ground. At the time, science fiction was not a popular film genre. And even though Lucas was coming off a huge success with his blockbuster, *American Graffiti*, studio after studio turned him down when he came to them with this very odd little script about little robots that beeped and binged and a large furry creature named Chewbacca.

> Trust your intuition and your heart—and you'll be lead towards accomplishments you never thought possible.

After four years of being told "no," Lucas was still not ready to give up, because he believed in this project with all his heart and soul. His intuition would not let him abandon it.

Finally, an executive at 20th Century Fox decided to roll the dice, if Lucas could make the film for the right budget. And of course, the rest is film history. The original *Star Wars* trilogy grossed over 2.4 billion dollars since their release in 1977, and now, more films in the franchise are being made than ever before. It's only because Lucas trusted himself and his ability, despite rejection after rejection, that his Star Wars Empire exists to this day.

Lucas' story (and that of so many other people) proves the central idea behind this chapter—trust yourself once and for all, because you and only you have what it takes to reinvent your life! This is your unique journey and the gifts that will result from reinventing yourself anew; only you can bring to the world.

As you make your way on your life reinvention, there is no question you will face occasional bouts of self-doubt. Now is the perfect time to take control of those episodes and stop doubting your ability to transform your life. You are responsible for the progress you have made thus far. You have earned the right to trust yourself!

7 Strategies to Promote Trusting Yourself

Inner Forte's 7 Habits for Reinventing and Reigniting Your Life are your best strategies that will help you promote trust in yourself, your business and in all areas of life.

1. Avoid comparison with others

For one moment, imagine your path as a garden. You may admire the garden of another and even visit from time to time, but their garden is not the same as or superior to your own. Trust that you know exactly how much and how often to water your own garden and allow yourself to bloom in your own unique way.

2. Accept that you are enough

No one else could have walked the path you have walked; you know that now. Trust that this is true on the continuing path of your reinvention. Every day, assert the following words with full conviction:

I am enough, I have enough, and I do enough!

3. Accept the perfection in the process

The tendency toward perfectionism can easily lead to self-doubt and discouragement. Acknowledging this empowers you to enjoy the process of your reinvention and trust that the progress that you make is enough.

4. Be fully engaged

Your mind and body crave activity. If you make a habit of moving your body and engaging your mind on the path of your reinvention, you will continue to learn from each new experience or thought you have. Trust that your energy is best spent in engaging fully in your transformation.

5. Give yourself credit for accomplishments

Be free with praise for your ongoing achievements while you continue your reinvention. Now is not the time for false humility or belittling yourself. You are navigating a course to success; you are blazing your own trail as you were meant to. Own that you have The Power to Reinvent Your Life, and trust that your accomplishments are worthy of praise.

6. Practice self-acceptance and forgiveness

You are making a journey into the unknown; there are bound to be a few setbacks. It is not an indication that you are untrustworthy; it is simply how life works. Accept these setbacks as opportunities to grow and gain wisdom and forgive yourself for any disappointments. Trust that through acceptance and forgiveness, your path toward success will continue to become more apparent.

7. Reinvent your personal narrative

How do you tell yourself your own story? Do you hear your mind's voice telling a story of self- doubt—or your heart's voice telling a story of self-trust? Try to tune into your heart's version of your story. Your heart sees the lessons you've learned, the progress you've made, and the promise of your awesome reinvention journey.

Now that you learned to trust yourself, let it continue to lead to your next step with Confidence and Courage…

CHAPTER 5

Building Courage to Shake Off Setbacks

"Whereas Passion is the fire, courage is the force that propels you forward towards your greatness."

Yvonne Dayan

Courage is easy to define, more challenging to explain. By definition, courage is the choice or willingness to confront the very thing you fear.

Simple, right?

But try to explain what courage does, how it feels or what you must do to acquire it and you may find it's not so simple!

NATURE'S WAY

As a lover of nature, I see bamboo, one of nature's prime examples of resiliency and courage.

This noble grass starts life as a small rhizome, no bigger than the palm of your hand, planted in a piece of earth. From this humble beginning, bamboo shoots up, growing as fast as three feet in one day, up to nine feet in one year. From one small planting, an entire forest will grow.

When it is cut back, the bamboo will spring forth again, undeterred by the blade's edge.

Courage—once planted in the soul—grows rapidly and mightily, spreading until it is unstoppable. With courage, even the most demoralizing downturn can be transformed into an opportunity for growth and creating a positive outcome from a negative circumstance.

What is certain about courage is that it expands, frees, and empowers those who acquire and master it! That's why I will share my story about my bamboo plant along with 4 powerful lessons learned, which are crucial to propel the journey for any candidate for reinvention.

NATURE'S WAY TO BECOME UNSTOPPABLE

I remember bringing a rare type of red bamboo plant from Hawaii and trying to plant it in my backyard. I had all kinds of weather and environmental challenges, and it was taking a long time before I could see any sign of growth, therefore, after various attempts I was ready to abandon the project all together.

After asking around, I learned that *the requirement for bamboo shoots to show up above ground is that they first grow deep roots underground.* Knowing this, I did not give up, and waited until the tenacious plant finally bloomed.

Deepening Our Roots: Just like bamboo, we, too, have to deepen our roots and build the necessary courage for a successful outcome to blossom. Reinvention is a process; and we need to grow roots that are material, emotional as well as spiritual in nature;

We have to go deep before we can reach the heights we want to enjoy in our lives and careers.

We nourish our metaphoric roots by consistently removing obsessive and doubtful thoughts that deplete us, instead of filling up our minds with positive, fresh, energy-producing, and winning thoughts that bolster our courage.

- **Persevere**

    Don't be deceived if, getting back your health, creating more wealth, revamping your relationships, or everything else you are striving to achieve get delayed and don't show up immediately. Don't give up! Results may come slow, because they may be disguised or concealed for a while, but like in bamboo, rest assured the roots are growing and they will eventually appear. Just keep moving towards your dreams with faith and perseverance, and unexpectedly you will be amazed!

- **Small Steps**

  It takes courage and persistence to take small deliberate actions in the right direction each day. In spite of how the media is constantly bombarding us with messages of instant gratification and overnight results, when it comes to real success in life, it is the small, steady, consistent, and habitual actions what will move you closer to your reinvention goals. What's one thing you can do today to strengthen your courage?

- **Outer Appearances**

  Bamboo teaches us to not be fooled by outer appearances; what seems weak is usually strong, and the opposite is usually true, too. The strength from bamboo comes from its flexibility, from its perseverance, and not from stiff determination, or outer appearances. Staying flexible makes you strong and irresistible.

> "Life is like a plant. If you nourish it, it flourishes.
> Neglect it and it withers."
> Yvonne Dayan

You may not be the strongest, biggest or most famous but like bamboo, you have your own inner light. Be proud of who you are, stay strong, stay steady, and dare to let your own gifts shine. You know what those are…

YOU ARE BIGGER THAN YOUR CIRCUMSTANCES…AND SETBACKS

Setbacks, hard times, and downturns are bound to happen. Some will be simple to overcome, but others may knock you right off course. In either case, you will do wonders once you learn how to integrate in your consciousness this powerful principle to boost your courage.

You are bigger than your problems.

When you adopt this bold attitude, you enable yourself to stop fearing difficulties and, instead, learn how to use them to become stronger and more focused on your unique talents, and results you want to express through your reinvention.

Every time difficulties come about, do as the old song says, "Pick yourself up, dust yourself off, and start all over again." Stay focused on what you really want, and don't allow problems to distract you from achieving your ultimate vision. Instead, find workable solutions that will put you back on track.

Whether your goals are to reinvent your image, your fitness, your relationships, your career, or your lifestyle, there's always a choice to make things right, once you dare to believe and have the courage to follow your dreams.

There is a saying that God never gives us more than what we can handle. There is truth in that. And even when you feel like you've got more on your plate than you can deal with, it simply means you have the greatness within to conquer all those difficulties and the potential to grow beyond them and make amazing things happen for you and for other people in your world.

We live in an Absolute Compassionate Universe that insures each one of us individually can deal with whatever situations or setbacks come at us. You may not always feel this reassuring factor in your life, but it's there.

The fact that we can't see or feel something
doesn't mean it's not there.

Just look back at your life. When you connect the dots, you will find that this delicate balance has always been a reality and your potential for growth is ever present.

Every setback that you are faced with is there with one purpose; to move you away from where you are and get you closer to where your destiny needs you to be. To allow that process to work, however, you must believe you can overcome these situations!

To truly believe it, speak it, affirm it with courage right now: I am bigger than any situation, stronger than any setback, and more powerful than any problem.

NO FAILURES, ONLY FEEDBACK

There is no real failure, only feedback to help us reinvent our lives!

Every one of us has experienced failures; hindrances, stumbling blocks along life's path that can make following through a reinvention journey seem frightening.

> The more challenges we face in life, the more our potential increases for Greatness.

And yet, those impediments have prepared you to take this journey.

Maybe you've been working in an unfulfilling job for too long. Perhaps you've invested too much in a relationship with the wrong person, perhaps dieting hasn't produced the body fitness you expected. Whatever the reason, these kinds of disappointments can make you feel as if your life is stuck on repeat, because you're in a constant cycle of doing the same thing day after day with no real direction or purpose, or reward.

If the above rings familiar to you, take heart! You are not

chained to days already behind you. Yes, we may encounter, sadness, anger, fear, and hurt, but we also find love, joy, laughter, healing, compassion, acceptance, and gratitude for all lessons learned.

Every day we can discover more about ourselves and gather new information to renew our lives. Best of all, understanding your past does not define your future, yet it's the foundation of the courage you'll need for your next adventure.

Thanks to those so-called failures, you have gained wisdom that will help you redesign the kind of life you desire at this stage of your life. You are now better able to change the patterns that no longer serve your purpose and choose differently, more wisely than before. You can now harness the lessons of your past experiences to enable your discernment over what you need to change and what you must let go.

COURAGE IN PERSEVERANCE
The Art of Moving Forward

All disappointments are future appointments for
your reinvention strategies.

Reinvention necessitates acceptance and forgiveness of all past disappointments. This is important for three main reasons:

- Forgiving your past hurts allows you to let go of any fear or negativity associated with them
- Once that negativity is released, you can objectively gain the lessons you need to learn from those experiences.
- Gaining those lessons helps avoid making the same mistakes in the days to come.

Acceptance and forgiveness will grant you the courage to persevere in the face of future difficulties and feed your *Power to Reinvent Your Life*. When you do feel like giving up, when a setback has proven to be major, here is a three-step process to get your courage back and move on.

1. Learn

When faced with hindrances, become clear on your current values as they are now. Realize that everyone makes mistakes. Accept that the past is the past. Concentrate on any positive repercussions of the situation. Your openness in learning from an error gives you the ability to judge objectively and move forward.

Consider which assets you possess that served you well through those difficult times and which ones you might also use in similar situations to good effect.

2. Let Go

You must also take an honest look at the negative aspects of a situation. If something you did was the cause, take note, resolve not to make the same mistake, and then let it go. Dwelling on what has already occurred, and which you can no longer change, will just cause more hesitation on your part.

Make the decision to let go by expressing your hurt, as well as your responsibility for your part on the situation and in this way, you will not only eliminate self-blame and feeling like a victim, you will become free to really love yourself and others and move forward with courage.

When you're looking backward, you can't look forward, so give yourself permission to move on to the next step.

3. Next!

Finally, take a decisive step forward towards your next goal or your new experience, and make a bold informed choice about your future. Continue to learn from your experiences.

Whatever comes next for you, know that through any previous setbacks you've endured, you will now only add strength to your ability to persevere in your Reinvention path!

DEBUNKING YOUR "WHAT IFS"

The biggest thing that holds us back from taking risks is the fear that we will fail. It's all about those darn "What Ifs" — "What if I'm not good enough to do this?" "What if nobody supports me in this?" "What if I can't figure out how to get this done?"

Well, leave your "what if" at the door and give it a shot, whatever it is. You owe it to yourself to take the right calculated risks and risk failure. You will only learn from every experience.

> Just as evil is the absence of good,
> Fear is simply the absence of courage

You can steamroller your way over your "What Ifs" every time—by choosing COURAGE. When you choose courage, fear has no choice but to disappear. Allow your heart to fill with courage, fortitude, and love rather than to remain empty in fear.

It may help to ask yourself a whole different series of 'what if's.' Let me explain.

One evening I was in a restaurant with a few colleagues preparing for a talk I was scheduled to give. I had a clear idea about the topics I wanted to cover with them, but first, someone asked me an insightful question. "How do you begin to reinvent yourself? I am in great need to change many areas in my life, but I'm afraid of even starting. What if it doesn't work out?"

There it was. Her giant 'what if.' I could see it would hold her back if she didn't choose another way of viewing her situation.

Those two powerful words can mean the difference between procrastination and starting your transformation, depending on how you used them!

So, I flipped the script and answered her by saying, "Yes, what if? What if…?"

"What if …you surpass your expectations? "What if …you get promoted?

"What if…you get to your ideal weight and feel like a million bucks?

"What if …you connect with your ideal relationship?

"What if …you succeed at something you've always wanted to try?"

The room fell silent, as I asked one more 'what if.'

"What if it works out so well you wished you had started much earlier?"

But she still wasn't convinced. She came back with her Number One "what if."

"But what if I fail?"

"Well," I said, "Then you'll be in the same place you are today, except much wiser and much more experienced. So, even in failure, you succeed! And you may learn enough from your attempt to do it right the next time! Here's the real what if you need to ask. *"What if you never try?* Do you really want to let your opportunity to reinvent your happiness and success go by?"

My colleagues' eyes suddenly sparkled with enthusiasm. We continued to talk and, by the end of the evening, each one of them was eager to act with renewed courage and confidently tackle some of their important but forgotten projects and allow themselves the opportunity to embark in a reinvention journey that would lead them to discover a new level of encouragement in their most authentic Selves.

Every one of us has courage in our hearts. The secret to evoke it is having someone who can help us unlock it and empower us to face our fears and do the things that frighten us. In our seminars, people grow together and everyone benefits thanks to participants feeling the support and love in the room, and the courage becomes contagious. I love to see the shift in people's faces as the transformation magically occurs!

DEBUNKING YOUR "I CANT'S"

There is something else besides those 'what ifs' in the way of your passion and success.

How often have you found yourself second-guessing your decision-making ability, your potential, your level of skills and talents? How often have you caught yourself saying, "I'm just not good enough. I *can't.*"

Yes, the "I cant's" are just as paralyzing as the "What Ifs." It's a mindset that holds you back from really progressing and getting to your next level of success.

The moment you stop the 'I cant's,' the moment you stop making excuses for yourself and make the moves that are way overdue is the moment you take control of your life. We call that taking your power back. The moment you realize that you are the sole person responsible for the consequences in your life is the moment you rise and take control of who you are and the results you create.

When you accept ownership, you put yourself in a much better position to bring about a change in life. And that, friends, is the turning point in which your courage will *blossom.*

To jumpstart that important evolution in your development, stop focusing on your weakness. Stop second-guessing yourself.

Stop engaging in self-defeating behavior. Instead, switch to what is known as the *Strengths Approach*. A much more loving, supportive and energetic alternative to achieving and enjoying the things you want in life.

THE STRENGTHS APPROACH

In the Strengths Approach, you reevaluate yourself at this point in your development to discover where your core strengths lie and how you use them to deal with any given situation. Once learned, you can use this information whenever you need a boost in self-esteem, or to resolve difficulties that may arise in your reinvention journey.

To begin, embrace your Inner Forte—your set of natural strengths—and list the strengths that add power and forward momentum to your personality. Those might include such attributes as charm, loyalty, kindness, acceptance, warmth, adaptability, perseverance, enthusiasm, a quick mind, and a cool affect or strong emotions that connect with others. Once you undertake this self-evaluation, you will key in to these strengths and understand how they energize you and help you continually improve.

When you focus on your natural strengths, rather than obsess on your weaknesses, you give rise to that which makes you more powerful, rather than that which makes you weak and depletes your energy. In turn, that fuels you to reach your potential in life.

Yes, it's important to embrace your weaknesses and accept them as part of you, while at the same time improve on them to transform them into assets. It's all a part of this reinvention journey.

Another interesting phenomenon is that when you concentrate on your assets and build up your strengths, your weaknesses also tend to improve more quickly, and as a result, help to support you in your quest for realizing your ultimate vision.

I've often say to those who fault themselves for their inconsistencies that: "Weaknesses are really strengths that haven't found an outlet to shine!"

DELETING THE NEGATIVES

It is difficult, however, to entirely block out negatives. Life is sometimes full of them.

More distressingly, the world is full of people around telling us what we can and can't do. They may focus on your mistakes and failures, seemingly in an attempt to completely undermine whatever success you've enjoyed. Be aware it has nothing to do with you. It's more about them and how they deal with their own limitations, and their need for control.

> DELETE the negative energies and UPLOAD all the positive ones

That's why you need to condition yourself to automatically tune them out when they try to discourage you.

When it comes to your success, their opinions don't matter. At the end of the day, it just comes down to your capabilities, your skills, your capacity to embrace change, and your passion to succeed and make a difference in the world that determines your results—not what anyone else thinks.

Here's a living example of this truth. Dr. Kenneth Jaffe, originally of Park Slope, Brooklyn, spent 25 years as a family doctor. Fearing a loss of his independence in the U.S. health care system, he quit his lucrative career at the age of 55 and bought some farmland. Now he raises grass-fed beef without the use of antibiotics or hormones.

Dr. Jaffe's reinvention forced him to confront a new life doing work about which he knew nothing about, but he refused to let fear of the unknown, and other people's opinions, prevent him from trying it out. Dr. Jaffe ended up fulfilled by his work in sustainable agriculture and feels grateful for his new life. He and other farmers in the Catskills support the farm-to-school program and donate grass-fed beef to children from kindergarten all the way to 12th grade.

Emulate the courage of Dr. Jaffe and other men and women who embark on a journey into the unknown. Dare to take the necessary risks to excel on the path of your own personal reinvention!

7 Strategies to Build Your Courage and Conquer Your Fears

Remember that Love Overcomes Fear

When you learn to love yourself, you will also learn to trust the future you're reinventing yourself for. Run towards the good you love, yet have been afraid to attempt, and watch your fear disappear.

1. Faith Always Breeds Courage

Ask the Power of the Universe for guidance and reassurance, and you shall receive guidance and reassurance along your journey. The more you cultivate faith in your heart, the braver you'll feel about tackling the unknown.

2. Keep Your Dreams in Your Heart

Believe in the goals you feel most keenly inside you, goals that seem to come from your Higher Self. The inspiration of these heartfelt dreams is powerful enough to carry you forward towards them.

3. Step Out of Your Comfort Zone

The more you step out of your comfort zone, the more you avoid the 'same old' syndrome in your life, the more you will break free of attachments you no longer need and the more you will feel empowered to transform. When you're prepared to bear the discomfort of new risks, you grow in courage and are free to forge the future ahead.

4. Adopt the "I Can" Philosophy

By saying I *can*, believing in it, and constantly feeding yourself positive thoughts, you will change your mindset and feel courageous as you leap into action. Own your new *I can* attitude and tap into it daily; this will influence the people around you and bring you much prosperity along your journey.

5. Remember to Say "Thank You"

When you feel gratitude for all you've been given and all you may be able to achieve, you stay appreciative for your successes and motivated to gain more.

6. Have Patience

You are transforming your life but remember that this level of transformation does not happen overnight or without a few steps backwards in between the many steps forward. Hang in there and continue to find forward momentum. Remember bamboo? Your own progress will surprise you!

7. Keep the End of Your Journey at the Forefront of Your Mind

When you can see and 'feel' where you're going, it keeps you excited and stimulated to move forward. You don't focus on what you can't do—instead, you concentrate on how you can bring the anticipated pleasure and meaningfulness that you are creating through your reinvention journey, into every area of your life.

Courage builds up your reactivity, which awaits you in the next chapter!

CHAPTER 6

Getting Creative and Exploring New Possibilities

"You are here and no longer there! Get excited!"

Yvonne Dayan

You have reached the part of your reinvention journey which only you can define. Only you have the answers for what happens now.

Consider this step a blank page waiting for you to write the future of your story on it. Or perhaps a hidden glen of yet unseen possibility by human eyes. There is no preexisting text to edit, no travel-worn path to follow. No, you are the author here. You are the trailblazer.

Open your mind to your innate sense of curiosity and wonder. Look at the world around you. Can you see the limitless possibilities around you? Begin with a clear mind; a silent interior is open to receive ideas from the place in you where inquisitiveness and awe reside. Allow these thoughts to flow freely; don't limit yourself to what you already know. Your curiosity and creativity will lead you on the new and untrodden path that you will blaze during this part of your Reinvention.

You are here! Get excited!

Inspiration is the place on your journey where passion ignites. Give yourself permission to be curious and get creative. Explore possibilities that you would never have before, especially if you get anxious thinking about what's coming next. Lose your worries and enjoy every step of this part of your reinvention because you have earned it.

TRAVELLING LIGHT: EMBRACING THE WORLD OF POSSIBILITY

You no longer carry the extra baggage of past setbacks, fear of obstacles, or self-doubt. Because you've unpacked so much already on your Reinvention journey, you can travel light.

You'll find this leaves an open space inside you. Use this internal freedom to explore your world of possibility. *Becoming open to possibilities is empowering. It is an acknowledgment that no matter where you are in life, you are not a prisoner of your past or current circumstance.*

Living in the present and exploring what's possible for you

now allows you to infuse your reinvention journey with adventure, play, enthusiasm, passion, and experimentation.

At this point, your exploration will have you looking or trying different things to find out what's the perfect fit for your new self. You might not know whether a given solution will work until you actually try it out, so give it a go. And when you start venturing into new territory, keep a sense of adventure. Make it fun so that the vibrant inner child that's within you, full of curiosity, aliveness, and wonder, will get on board with your desires.

It is the child in you that attracts to you your heart's desires. Allow yourself an attitude of curiosity and be like an explorer.

When I talk about explorers, I can't help but think of the internationally-known underwater researcher, Jacques Cousteau. While he was training to become a pilot after his stint at the naval academy, he was in a serious automobile accident, which ended his aviation career. While swimming underwater with goggles, he had a breathtaking revelation—in the deep was where he truly belonged!

Thus began his love of the sea. In 1943, pursuing a way to explore under the oceans for longer periods of time, he teamed up with engineer Emile Gagnan and developed the SCUBA, or Self-Contained Underwater Breathing Apparatus. Now the world under the sea was open to all—and it might never have happened if Cousteau wasn't motivated to unlock his own personal passion of sea exploration.

> Each moment is new. Staying present in the "now" offers each of us fresh opportunities for Empowerment, Reinvention and Renewal

Of course, many explorers throughout history helped define

our world. Christopher Columbus made his first journey to the Caribbean Islands in 1492. He also made his four trailblazing voyages to the Americas. Jeanne Baré was the first woman to sail around the world. Baré circumnavigated the world in the 1700s, conducting research, gathering, and uncovering and array of new species of plants. Marco Polo made spearheading expeditions to Asia and China. His travels and writings helped to open up trade to the Far East to Europe. Amelia Earhart was the first female pilot to ever fly across the Atlantic Ocean. Earhart broke the woman's world altitude record reaching 14,000 feet. She set new standards, opening the way for other women who wanted to fly, Vasco de Gama was the first European to reach India by sea. De Gama made an innovative voyage to Calicut, India in 1498, travelling around the Cape of Good Hope in South Africa.

All of these women and men set out on journeys into the unknown. They had no idea what they would find. Many of their most important discoveries came about purely by accident. But they wouldn't have happened at all if these explorers hadn't embarked on voyages with very, very uncertain destinations!

Who knows the wonders you'll discover on yours?

When you apply an explorer's spirit to your reinvention, you'll find what you're looking for—yet it may be a totally surprising and delightful destination.

CREATIVITY—WHAT'S POSSIBLE TODAY?

Any part of you can become something new and wonderful, simply by being open-minded. Move freely and unburdened from possibility to possibility. Make mindful choices and accept the results.

Most importantly, move forward, allowing for innovation and curiosity. These are childlike qualities that perhaps you've gotten out of touch with in your adult life. If so, try and reignite the spirit you had when you were younger, feel the inspiration, awe, and wonder, and let them dance in your heart.

Try this: For a moment, allow yourself to search for the spirit of the inner child that still resides within you.

Can you recall how big the world seemed when you were a child, and how each discovery filled you with awe and inspiration?

If you can bring that feeling back, and get reacquainted with those emotions, you will fan the flames of your passions and feel the power of rejuvenating your Self.

Bring that same spirit into exploring new ways of living and working that will bring you joy and fulfillment.

> Nothing in life is a failure. Believe instead each mistake is an opportunity to evolve, and your path will be one creative adventure.

Discover unusual ways you can contribute to the world around you. Begin by arousing your innate curiosity and asking yourself how you can change your status quo and infuse new passion into different areas of your life.

Here's my 'out of the box' list of things you could explore!

- Research other careers
- Revamp current roles
- Learn more about your or others' industries
- Seek alternative professional or social networks
- Grow your finances
- Get in shape
- Remake your image
- Increase enthusiasm in your business

- Deepen and improving your relationships
- Boost your health
- Start a charitable endeavor
- Give or ask for a grant to start a project
- Start a new hobby
- Learn to dance or play an instrument
- Take time out to play, laugh, love, and share with friends
- Engage in the art of non-doing-ness for a day
- (Add your own categories!)

In other words, step out of your daily routine and look at it as an interested observer. Objectively analyze how you can increase the light and joy in your life right now, remembering that life is a blank canvas where you can paint the future of your choice. Approach it with all the passion and excitement of a child on their birthday. On that day, everything is possible for a child—the world of opportunity is wide open, and magic can happen!

Allow yourself to trust that your ideal path will unfold before you. You just have to be willing to take that first step.

Ask yourself the next two questions to jumpstart your creativity and explore new passions:

- If money were not an issue, what would you do with your life?
- What's the most important thing that motivates you to spring out of bed with enthusiasm each day? (Besides coffee)

The answers might lead you in some very interesting directions.

BOBBY'S ACCOMPLISHED GOALS

(Case Study 3)

My friend Bobby came to my course tired and dissatisfied with his working life because he had to travel overseas constantly. All the time he could have spent with his wife, kids and grandkids was slipping away and it was time he could never get back again.

He reached his limit and finally, was no longer willing to trade a salary for that precious time, so he was ready to change up his career of 20 years. But when he began to consider the possibility of building his own career from home, the prospect scared him and filled him with doubt. Partly because he was taught for years to hold a good job with a steady pay and retirement account, or he risked his entire financial future. Being self-employed and working from home made him feel like he was like walking a tightrope without a net.

With the training and recommendations we gave to Bobby, he saw things in a different light and fear could no longer stop him. In fact, it energized him and filled with new energy, because for the first time in years, he was excited about building a business of his own from scratch—it really lit a fire in him.

Among other things, we taught him to set short medium and long term goals… and to realize them gradually, to set some really small goals and to celebrate with his family as he conquered each milestone. His entire family ended up rooting for him, so they all monitored his progress and his setbacks together, and he began to build victories that all of them could enjoy together.

His first win, once he reached his first financial goal, was taking the whole family on a weekend cruise. His wife got the attention she needed, the kids got to enjoy themselves, and that, in turn, encouraged him to push forward.

His goals progressively got bigger, his rewards more fulfilling, and he never lost track of his targets. He had more time with family and was expanding his creativity in a way that his work would be more meaningful. Soon, he had built an online business that made him a five-figure income. He was able to employ two assistants to help him out. And all this happened at the end of only his first year!

The secret? First, he created an atmosphere of complete acceptance and approval from his family, which gave him the stability he needed. Second, he surrounded himself with unconditionally loving and supportive friends he met during our Inner Forte seminar and got the coaching he needed which encouraged him on. Third, he was realistic enough to know he couldn't make millions right off the bat. Instead, he started small, saw what worked and what didn't, made adjustments and took his accomplishments to the next level.

Too many people set huge, intimidating goals and find that, weeks later when they're nowhere near those goals; they're deflated and depressed. They give up even though they may have been making some significant progress.

For Bobby, the secret was taking it step-by-step, and having the right support. It would be very helpful to have some loving cheerleaders behind you; giving you the encouragement and support you need.

CREATIVITY
Allow New Ideas to Flourish

This part of your reinvention is all about opening up your thought process, so that your mind can become a more creative and fertile breeding ground for new ideas that will motivate and excite you. Cultivating childlike wonder and spontaneity are perfect for this phase!

To illustrate my point, I'll use a story of how a child's mind brilliantly and creatively interpreted the workings of the Body-Mind-Spirit connection.

Years ago, on a spring day, I was walking around a beautiful golf course surrounded by beautiful foliage bordering on a lake, with my very good friend Angie. We were discussing the connection between mind and body and how negative emotions can affect us in harmful ways.

That's when her son Michael, who was walking with us and listening closely, jumped in. He was all of five years old.

"Mom," he said to Angie "I think I know how this works." "Really?" she asked with amused eyes. "How?"

"Well," he replied, "When a person is angry and has bad feelings, and they keep the bad feelings inside themselves for a long time, those bad feelings make a ball, a small ball, maybe the size of a Ping-Pong ball, in their heads."

"Wow. Then what happens?" asked Angie.

"Well…if they keep feeling angry, that Ping-Pong ball grows to the size of a basketball!"

"And if they *still* feel bad and mad, then the ball gets so big, the head doesn't have room for it, so it throws it back down into the body. Where it lands, that's where the person gets sick!"

I thought to myself, "Not bad. The kid's onto something!"

This story perfectly illustrates how looking at the world through the eyes of a child gets you thinking outside the box.

I found Angie's response and her creative discourse to be very representative of a dynamic that allows our minds to engage the imagination, rather than the usual dynamic we mostly encounter in our society that shuts down our creative innovative minds.

Usually, we think of a strange and new approach to something and instantly our adult mind tells us we're crazy to consider it.

But maybe what we've just thought of is a new way to get something done, like how to take care of our body-mind connection!

So, don't dismiss out of hand an idea that's unusual or even seems too preposterous. Instead, allow your creativity to explore that idea and see if there's something to it. This is how you find new and surprising solutions for challenges you would have once avoided.

In other words, don't just allow yourself to see the obstacles standing between you and your passion. Instead, look for the solutions to overcome them. In this way, obstacles transform into stepping-stones that allow you to make progress.

Allowing yourself to embrace childlike curiosity and creativity adds significantly to the enjoyment you'll experience on your reinvention journey.

As you pass through this phase, you'll find you are now excitingly close to the goals you envisioned for yourself. As your passion continues to inspire you onward, your inner child's curiosity and creativity will keep you motivated and help you embrace each new possibility.

Enjoy this amazing part of your life's path and relish the anticipation of meeting your most wanted outcome very soon!

If you feel as though you've lost your inner child's enthusiasm to explore and create, here are some strategies to help you bring that all- important aspect of yourself to the forefront, so it can aid you in calling forth your Power of Reinvention.

7 Strategies for Empowering Your Inner Child's Curiosity and Creativity

1. Awaken Your Inner Child's Intuition

Give your rational mind time to rest and, at the same time, allow your instinctive spirit freedom to be curious. Explore each new thought, considering only the positive aspects of each.

2. Get Moving

Your inner child is like most children—it rarely sits still. Instead, it wants to explore, play, and move from one thing to the next more quickly than most of us can think. So let it do just that! Activity stimulates endorphins and mental acuity and will help your curiosity blossom.

3. Quit Overanalyzing!

Rational thought is, of course, a useful tool, but right now your intuition needs you to pay attention to it. Follow your instincts and 'listen' to your emotional reactions. Just as children know when to curb their curiosity or let it run free, your inner child naturally knows how to draw the best options to you, primarily because they pay close attention to what their instincts tell them.

4. Live in the Question

Like most kids, your inner child is naturally curious. It is this inquisitiveness that allows your imagination to soar. If you are wondering about something, learn more about it. Don't let go of your questions; instead, explore to answer them!

5. Relish Your Innate Confidence

Watch how children play. They rarely question themselves. Instead, they allow themselves to do whatever interests them and stimulates their creativity. The inner child in you will also follow where curiosity leads, because it, too, has innate self-confidence and freedom from worry.

6. Be Enthusiastic About Knowing More

Every time you discover something or have an 'a-ha!' moment, allow yourself to get excited for your discovery. Encouraging your childlike enthusiasm will help you bridge boredom, self-pity, and other negative emotions.

7. Enjoy Yourself and Have Some Fun

Your inner child, of course, loves adventure. Travel around; visiting different countries or even a few unfamiliar neighborhoods can really expand your perspective. Continue to broaden your imagination by doing other new and different things you find you enjoy.

Commitment changes everything. It lets you ride the wave of your reinvention creatively, courageously, peacefully, joyfully, while you stick to your guns and reach your desired destination.

Guess what's next? Commitment!

CHAPTER 7

Committing to Seeing Your Reinvention Through

"Commitment is the key to form habits that exude
and define your Greatness"
Yvonne Dayan

You are energized and confident; you are prepared to act on the ideas you've been feeding your mind and soul. You are excited, and you should be! Be mindful that distractions can eat away at your aspirations. Therefore, reinvention requires a firm commitment to seeing it through. Consider the following scenario to help you continue firmly invested in yourself and in your success.

Think about a time when you achieved a valuable goal, something you really wanted that still now, when you think about it, you smile with satisfaction and pride.

What was your level of commitment?

How far were you willing to go to get your results?

Were you determined? Or were you okay giving it a try and seeing if by a fluke, maybe things could work out?

Your answers will reveal the disparity between the different attitudes towards commitment. When you are determined, you make things a priority in your life. When you are not, you do things only when they feel comfortable to you.

If you want to be successful at reinventing any area of your life, you need to be committed to take action. If you only want to make a fleeting change to get by, then a commitment is not so essential.

Commitment is like a promise you make to yourself, and it's central to creating the personal and professional prosperity and abundance you project into every area of your reinvention.

Sometimes I ask myself how people can prosper and find fulfillment without being committed to something, whether it is to relationships, to their life's work, to serving and contributing to others, improving herself or himself, or any other worthy cause.

Once you reaffirm your commitment to your reinvention, your actions flow easily, naturally, seemingly effortlessly, and they end up speaking louder than words. With these benefits in mind, here is an excellent thought-provoking question that will help you explore your level of commitment:

What goals are you committed to accomplish through your reinvention?

With your commitment in place, now is the time to focus on translating your vision into deliberate ACTION. Because ACTION is POWER!

Here are a few examples of simple reinvention goals and the

action-based activities needed to accomplish them; for example, for:

- **Growing your income**

  Commit to get creative and find out about new investments that may be available or investigate about opportunities to invest with others.

- **Revamping your wardrobe**

  Commit to look for sales and cost- effective options for your favorite fashion items.

- **Getting new clients**

  Commit to joining a new club or place that centers around an interest of your clients.

- **Transcending losses**

  Commit to get out of isolation and join a group where people don't need to be afraid to publicly express their feelings, and their desires to transcend to their next level. Commit to open up and share how much what (or who) you've lost.

- **Reigniting your passion**

  Commit to create a time each week dedicated to breaking out of your comfort zone and trying something new.

ALIGN YOUR INTENTIONS WITH YOUR BEHAVIOR!

As you do begin to bring your desires to life, remember to follow through on what you want to accomplish by acting in the spirit of those objectives.

For example, let's say your areas of preference are centered on becoming financially successful. If you approach a goal of that nature by waking up around noon each day and spending your money recklessly without rhyme or reason, those riches you're after are probably going to be a bit elusive. That's why you need to cultivate actions that support your desires and not contradict them.

I have a student and friend named Jenna, whose goal was to attract the right romantic partner into her life. Even though she was shy and a bit of a loner, she was absolutely willing to get out of her shell and make time to meet people. She also made the effort to tweak her personality, so she appeared to be more outgoing to everyone that she met.

For her, those were the right moves. She aligned her actions with the goals she was committed to achieve, and in the process, reinvented her relationship status. Within a year, she was very happily married and now she has the best of both worlds. She leads a quiet, nature- centered and healthy lifestyle that she loves, and she shares her life with the loving husband that she wanted.

You, too, can enjoy that kind of positive outcome when you are committed to your reinvention, and take the action steps to support your ultimate goal. It also takes cultivating the right kind of habits that can support your commitment for your vision to come to life.

CREATING GOAL-DIRECTED HABITS

Habits are the building blocks to achieving success in any area of your choice. Interestingly, it isn't really goals that get you to your destination, it is your habitual ways of acting, feeling, and thinking while you are on the road to reinvention what get you there.

When I was a teenager, I would go to my grandmother, who passed away at 105 years old, may God bless her soul, to talk to her and try to get an understanding and perhaps some insight about what was going on in my life.

And my grandmother would pragmatically reply, "My child, stay focused. Complete one mission before you start another, and you will always succeed."

She was right! Instead of completing one task, I would move on to the next and continue with the same failing habits all over again.

Negative habits are destructive, and they take you down. Positive habits? Well, they eliminate non-essentials and prevent wasting time, allow you to create and maintain good relationships, they motivate, and in other words they build you up.

Next, I'll share some basic, yet vital habits to definitely take on board as you continue to harness the Power to Reinvent Your Life.

POSITIVE HABITS FOR SUCCESS

- **Carrying yourself with confidence**

  This practice is crucial to your overall success. The people you meet need to know you are confident in yourself and feel self-assured to carry things through with confidence.

- **Punctuality**

  Reflects appreciation for other people's time when you value it enough to honor your commitment. When you're on time, you demonstrate responsibility and show respect for others' schedules.

- **Self-care**

  Working out, dressing well, eating healthfully, and getting enough rest help keep you strong, focused and alert. If these habits aren't already a part of your reinvention routine, introducing them now is a great idea.

- **Showing respect for others and yourself**

  People will respond more and support you more readily if you demonstrate this quality. You also show respect for yourself when you follow your own time commitments.

- **Showing appreciation**

  You've learned to have gratitude for everything in your life, now express it and you'll find more good things coming your way. Realize that no one likes a complainer, and everyone likes someone who's humble and feels thankful for what they have.

- **Staying in the now**

  It is the only time over which you have control. If you find yourself obsessing over the past, well, realize it's over and done with, so just let go. If you obsess over the future? Then you might miss important things happening right this minute. My best advice: *Stay focused on The Present. The Point of Power to Reinvent your Life*.

Each of the above habits will make your reinvention journey more enjoyable, fun, gratifying and will make achieving your goals likely. Anecdotally speaking, once I took my grandmother's advice and developed new successful habits, I experienced pleasing results and much better outcomes!

INSPIRATION IS VITAL TO YOUR REINVENTION COMMITMENT

Imagine you are looking at a bird's eye view of the map for your reinvention journey. Can you see it in your mind from that high place?

If you can, trace that journey from the moment you realized you needed a reinvention, to the first steps along the path where you found your courage and let go of disappointments, moving forward into as you gained confidence and strength.

Just beyond those landmarks is your place of inspiration.

Your reinvention journey has been an awakening to what inspires you. This step is where you will discover what I often hear surprises people the most. Once you have reached the inspiration stage, you realize that reinventing yourself anew is so pleasing that you are living in the flow, enjoying a higher level of success, joy and passion, so much so that it causes many people to decide to continue reinventing themselves and rolling updated versions of who they are for the rest of their lives! And that's a wonderful decision to make. It means you have truly committed to improving yourself on an ongoing basis.

This is a result of your tapping into your endless well of inspiration, a well available to all of us, if we're willing to dig in and discover its stimulating waters of wonder. Which will in turn leave us questioning, "Why didn't I do this before?"

> Inspiration—the spiritual FORCE that stimulates the mind, drives emotions, and propels new and creative ACTION.

Let's examine my definition of inspiration for a moment. Within my definition are three distinct items that will add vitality to your commitment to reinvention: mental stimulation, experiencing emotion, and doing something creative.

Let's look at each element in turn:

1. Stimulate Your Mind

Over the course of this journey, you have trained your mind to seek new horizons. You have continued to push the boundaries of your previously held misconceptions and absorbed new ideas.

You have taught yourself to love learning about new things that may lead to other opportunities.

Your mind is like a sponge. When starved of ideas it grows dry and brittle, it hardens and is inflexible. You have allowed the water of free thought to create a pliant and flexible environment in your mind. The mental stimulation you are now capable of will be the wellspring of creativity from which ideas for your continued reinvention will flow.

2. Feel your Feelings

Strong emotions and passions are always triggered by your new creations.

> It's tough to stop someone who is driven from within!

For example, that feeling of excitement you experience when you are about to embark on a new adventure, or of accomplishment when you reach one of your cherished goals. The sense of acceptance when you realize your plans must change, or the courage you must demonstrate in order to withstand feelings all feed into your inspiration.

Because you have learned the art of moving forward while honoring your emotions, your reinvention journey will continue with balanced purpose, drawing inspiration from integrating thought and feeling as you continue your way towards reinvention.

3. Do Something Creative

You have already committed many creative acts, although you may not know it. Your journey has been fraught with choices and actions directed by you. You have, through your Power of Reinvention, created the most authentic version of yourself that you have ever known.

In this way, you might call your entire process more of an awakening to the inspiration you didn't even know you had.

Continue to create. Remember that whatever draws you to exploration and creativity is calling to that inner part of you that is always growing in understanding and continues to reach for authenticity. Your creative activity draws you closer to understanding the core of who you are. It is a journey that will take you places you never dreamed of, and because people change over the course of life, you will continue to surprise yourself as you keep moving forward on your path.

TAKE ACTION
Activate Your Reinvention Vision

"To unleash your vast potential, Act! Action will reveal more about you than the loftiest ideals"
Yvonne Dayan

Now that you've made it this far, it's time to act on your newfound freedom and inspiration and embark on your journey to reinvention!

What should your first steps be? How can you be sure you're truly in touch with your Source? What if some aspects of your personality are still holding you back?

Sometimes it's necessary to seek help with these questions. Behind some of the most successful entrepreneurs, movie stars, politicians, athletes and other successful people who have fulfilled their purpose and achieved their dreams are immensely gifted coaches.

This is a truth that you can trace all the way back to 300 BC! The legendary conqueror Alexander the Great had his own personal coach, a philosopher just as famous as Alexander! That man was Aristotle and he helped guide Alexander in using his strengths and understanding his weaknesses, so much so that Alexander said of him, *"I am indebted to my father for living, but to my teacher for living well."*

Becoming involved with a coach and a support group can definitely be a big assist to your advancement. We are social beings, and we thrive when we feel supported, accepted, approved, encouraged, and nurtured in the right way by our leaders, our families and our peers.

Your support team will come in handy when things get tough—which is bound to happen in any type of adjustment.

They will also redirect your path correctly whenever you veer off course. The key is to ensure that you have found the perfect balance between dependence and independence.

Also remember to research your desired destinations. There are many avenues of information that you may not have considered:

- The internet is an excellent resource. It has a wide variety of information and resources to help you get going.
- Newspapers, magazines, and periodicals may be waning in popularity, but don't discount them altogether. Depending on what you're looking for, they might have what you need; check them out.
- When all else fails, ask around. People who have expertise in the areas you're interested in exploring are happy to help. Word of mouth is still an excellent source of aid.

Once you have researched enough to know where to begin, get

going. Remember, you are worth every new beginning on this part of your journey. Your new experiences will be ones to learn from and treasure—you can view them as the sweet fruits of your reinvention.

Keep taking action, and you too may experience the joy of never-ending inspiration that will motivate you to continue a lifelong reinvention adventure that will draw you ever closer to being the most authentic, amazing, fabulous, version of yourself!

SUPPORT WHEN YOU NEED IT MOST

You've heard it before. Challenges are bound to come up and test your commitment to see your transformation through. These are a natural part of any life-changing course of action. Don't let setbacks discourage you.

Consider the fledgling bird, making its first few attempts at flight. It is the bird's destiny to fly, and it knows instinctively that it must. But even birds have teachers that push them encouragingly and show them how to soar.

Sometimes all it takes to keep going on your path is a helping hand. Our experienced mentors take great pleasure in helping you continue your transformation and remain committed to your success. We understand the path you are on. We were once there, and our joy is in offering you the extra tools you need to experience your reinvention to the fullest, and it is our privilege to help you along the way.

Your journey is as unique and beautiful as you are, and we feel grateful to help in your ultimate success.

7 Strategies for Bringing Success and Joy Into Your Reinvention Journey

This book has discussed all the effort that needs to go into a successful reinvention.

Let us be mindful, however, not to forget that joy should always be an integral part of everyday life. Here are 7 Reinvention Strategies to make sure you remain committed to your success and that you enjoy the journey towards your destination.

1. Appreciate Yourself and Your Efforts

Love, accept and approve of yourself every step of the way for exactly who you are right now, and where you are in your journey. Appreciation enhances your personality, relationships, health, and career, making you more attractive to others, and self-motivated. It multiplies everything you touch and draws abundance to your life.

Celebrate each triumph and each victory; savor the sweet fruits of your reinvention no matter how big or small you think they are. They are all valuable, and each is indispensable to your ultimate success.

2. Remain Humble

You were born to be real, not perfect! Sometimes, people get into the habit of thinking they have all the answers they need. No one ever does. Accept that and remain open to listen to other people's ideas and recommendations. That does not mean you have to agree with them or even take those suggestions, but it does mean you consider your options. You never know when someone will have an idea that will make things easier and more functional, ultimately helping you arrive at your goal more efficiently.

3. Cultivate Lasting Relationships

To attract lasting relationships, ensure that people feel good in your presence by maintaining a positive attitude, and you will attract and create satisfying relationships that will support and empower you to see your reinvention goals through.

Make people feel like a million bucks. The way people feel about you is a reflection of how you make them feel. If you make someone feel valuable, interesting, confident, sexy, lovable or intelligent when you're around, they're going to like you. If they feel insignificant, clumsy, boring, or unattractive around you…well, you won't see much of them in the future!

4. Live Long with Humor by Ignoring Rumors

Keep your humor sensor on. In every situation there is humor, all we need is to realize it and utilize it. Naysayers /rumors, discouragement/ rumors. Remember this: Live long with humor by ignoring the rumors!

5. Continue Learning

Make education a lifelong experience. Maybe you want to return to school full time, take an occasional evening class, just study on your own, or attend our seminar where you can meet like-minded people who also wish to reinvent themselves. Whatever suits you best, continue to grow your intellect and find out more about subjects you find interesting

6. Seek a Reinvention Coach

A reinvention life coach can help with many facets of your journey, including:

- Reinventing your career
- Reinventing your love life
- Reinventing your life's purpose
- Achieving challenging goals
- Creating prosperity
- Creating more free time in your life
- Getting your body back in shape
- Starting a new business

Your reinvention coach is also your cheerleader. Life is easier when someone is in your corner. When you know you have expert support, it's easier to take risks and chase after big goals.

Your life coach will also push you when you need it. They've seen plenty of clients attempt to avoid exactly what they need most for their success. They'll know when you're just being complacent and get you going and motivate you to succeed and start living at your highest level of being.

Most of us weren't formally taught how to live successfully. A life and career coach can help you to figure out what you want to do with your life, set goals, and achieve them. They have experience in helping others to live successful and fulfilling lives.

7. Relax! Trust The Universe To Handle the Details

Have you ever realized what a waste of time and energy worry is?

Worrying stresses you out and can make you age prematurely. It also takes up valuable time, time you could spend on solutions to your problems instead of being obsessed, and distracted by them.

Think about it. 90% of your worries never come to pass. So why let them haunt you?

Instead, relax, breathe deeply, and be happy knowing that the Universal Source of Goodness has your back and will handle all the details of your life. Stay in contact with your Source. Knowing that with all unknown mysteries, this is still a wonderful world.

Smile and others will absorb your positive energy and the good vibes emanating from you. Share the love and spread the joy of the "new you" all around. *Be that beacon of light you were meant to be! And above all, live your Forte!*

CONCLUSION

Congratulations for completing the book! You are awesome! You have proven that you are committed to advancing your own self, to enjoying the best life has to offer and to giving your best to the world and to those you love!

With that in mind, I'd like to recommend that you take the next step towards your growth and evolution and take advantage of my online course:

The Power to Reinvent Your Life Online Course
21 Keys to Jumpstart Your Passion, Purpose and Success!

For more information, please visit us at
http://reinventcourse.innerforte.com.

This course will guide you step-by-step through 21 high-level lessons to activate your potential and keep your life ever exciting, uncovering new levels of passion and success. These lessons will help you embrace the new you and stay motivated to be your best, have the best, and always attract the best to your life as you reach that special place where you can continuously prosper outrageously, love abundantly, and heal your life.

As you work your way through this course, I will personally have the privilege to interact with you, motivate you, coach and challenge you to break through the clutter, remove obstacles and step into your greatness.

"THANK YOU" for being committed to improving your life and reading this book, and receive my warmest "WELCOME" to our Inner Forte Family. Until we meet, I wish you joy and happiness and the best of luck in the successful pursuit of your reinvention mission.

May you always prosper outrageously, love abundantly, and

"LIVE YOUR FORTE!"

ABOUT THE AUTHOR

Speaker, gifted author, psychologist, and master trainer, Yvonne is a pioneer in the field of human potential. Her expertise in Reinvention seminars and coaching has helped thousands achieve success breakthroughs in their personal development, health, happiness emotional excellence, and wealth creation.

As an accomplished trainer with various degrees in psychology and counseling, Yvonne is often sought by the media as an expert and spokesperson in the fields of success and social behavior. She has appeared internationally on numerous TV and radio programs, in magazines and newspapers and was featured in the documentary movie: *Anything But Ordinary: Ordinary People Extraordinary Lives.*

In 2005, Yvonne produced the acclaimed DVD Series *Creating Your Own Fountain of Youth*, *Bringing Down the Light* and *Restoring Your Soul to Wholeness.* That created a paradigm shift in the way we can use our mind-body connection to impassion and heal our lives.

She has also appeared with Harrison Ford and Kristin Scott Thomas in the movie *Random Hearts*. She is a bestselling co-author of the book *Change Agents* with Brian Tracy, and most recently co-author of *SuccessOnomics* with Steve Forbes.

Driven by principle, Yvonne's greatest passion is dedicating her life to empowering people to unleash their highest potential. She specializes in coaching entrepreneurs, especially women, who are ready to prosper outrageously, love more abundantly, and lead extraordinary lives.

Yvonne has been leading her *InnerForte*™ and *Imastery*™ transformational programs for over 25 years, incorporating unique life-changing techniques. She actively teaches her innovative seminars in major teaching centers around the world.

To find out more about how Yvonne can help you Reinvent Yourself, visit her directly at www.YvonneDayan.com

✉ info@innerforte.com
f YvonneDayan1
🄾 Yvonnedayan1
in Yvonnedayan
🐦 Yvonnedayan1

www.InnerForte.com

OTHER WORKS FROM YVONNE DAYAN

Coming from Yvonne Dayan in 2020:

Reinvent Your Life "Wisdom and Affirmation Cards"

Reinvent Your Life "On Line Course & Webinar Series"

Yvonne's new book: *Inner Forte™ The Force Within*

Other Books:

Bestselling co-author of the book *Change Agents* with Brian Tracy.

Co-author of *SuccessOnomics* with Steve Forbes.

Available at Innerforte.com

DVDs:

Creating Your Own Fountain of Youth

Bringing Down the Light

Restoring Your Soul to Wholeness

Available Wholesale: Devorss & Company, New Leaf Distributing Company, innerforte.com

Retail: amazon.com, innerforte.com

Seminars:

Reinvent You 1-Day Seminar.

Inner Forte™ 3-Day Seminar.

To attend one of our *InnerForte™ Signature Seminars*, or to hire Yvonne to speak at your event please email us at: info@innerforte.com. 1-877-522-9642.

www.innerforte.com